Table of Contents

Part I - The Career Crossroads — 1

Chapter 1: The AI Age and Your Career — 2
- What the Research Says — 3
- 7-Step Survival Plan — 5
- Why This Matters Now — 7
- Do This Now: Kickstart Your Adaptability — 9

Chapter 2: The Automation Shockwave — 10
- Tasks Before Jobs: The First Wave of Change — 11
- How Fast Is It Coming? — 12
- Separating Hype from Reality — 15
- Impact Across Industries — 17
- Do This Now: Adapt to AI's Impact — 23

Chapter 3: The New Rules of Work — 25
- The Task Exposure Lens: Why the Same Job Can Be Safe or Risky — 26
- 10 At-Risk Job Categories — 28
- Top 10 Resilient Job Categories — 37
- Role-Mapping Pivot Exercise: Find Your Path to Resilience — 47
- Do This Now: Future-Proof Your Role — 51

Bonus Extras — 54

Part II - The 7 Steps to Future-Proof Your Career — 55

Chapter 4: Step 1 Future-Proof Mindset — 56
- Fast Learning Path: Building Adaptability & Resilience — 61
- Do This Now: Adaptability & Resilience — 62

Chapter 5: Step 2 Upgrade Constantly — 65
- Fast Learning Path: Embracing Lifelong Learning — 71
- Do This Now: Lifelong Learning & Upskilling — 73

Chapter 6: Step 3 AI + You — 76

Fast Learning Path: Becoming an
AI-Augmented Professional — 80

Do This Now: Leverage AI for Career Growth — 81

Chapter 7: Step 4 Work Smarter with AI — 84

Fast Learning Path: Supercharging Your Productivity with AI — 91

Do This Now: Daily AI Productivity Boost — 93

Chapter 8: Step 5 Double Down on Human Skills — 97

Fast Learning Path: Strengthening Key Human Skills — 105

Do This Now: Sharpen Your Human Edge — 107

Chapter 9: Step 6 Build Your Brand and Network — 111

Fast Learning Path: Expanding Your Network and Visibility — 119

Do This Now: Boost Your Network & Brand Today — 121

Chapter 10: Step 7 Career Agility — 125

Fast Learning Path: Cultivating Career Agility — 132

Do This Now: Boost Your Agility Today — 135

Part III - The Next 90 Days and Beyond — 138

Chapter 11: Your 90-Day Career Change Plan — 139

30/60/90-Day Roadmap — 140

Networking Strategy — 144

Upskilling Pathways — 146

Quick Wins & Low-Cost Options — 149

Do This Now: Your Action Plan — 151

Chapter 12: The Opportunity Window — 153

Why Now Is the Best Time to Act — 154

Historical Parallels — 156

Spotting and Seizing AI-Driven Opportunities — 159

Long-Term Positioning — 162

Do This Now: The Opportunity Window — 166

References — 170

Bonus Resources — 173

THE AI CAREER BOOK

A Step-by-Step Guide to Career Change Success in the AI Economy

LJ CUNNINGHAM

© Copyright 2025 - All Rights Reserved to LC Cunningham

No part of this book may be reproduced, duplicated, stored, or transmitted in any form or by any means without prior written permission from the author or publisher.

Legal Notice:

This book is protected by copyright and intended for personal use only. No portion may be modified, distributed, resold, quoted, or paraphrased without explicit written consent from the author or publisher. The author and publisher assume no responsibility for any errors, omissions, or outcomes resulting from the use of this material.

Disclaimer:

The information in this book is provided for educational and informational purposes only. While every effort has been made to ensure accuracy and reliability, no warranties are expressed or implied. The content should not be considered legal, financial, or professional advice. Readers are encouraged to seek guidance from qualified professionals before acting on any information contained herein.

By reading this book, you agree that the author and publisher are not liable for any loss, injury, or adverse outcome resulting from the application or misuse of the information provided.

Part I

THE CAREER CROSSROADS

Chapter 1
The AI Age and Your Career

Monday, 7:30 AM, 2025. Ethan, a 22-year-old recent graduate, checks his email for responses to the many jobs he applied to over the weekend. He's anxious. Rumor has it many companies now use Artificial Intelligence (AI) software to scan resumes and hold initial video interviews. *Did an algorithm decide my fate while I slept?*

Across town, Priya, a marketing manager with 12 years of experience, walks into a meeting. Her CEO is announcing a new AI platform to *"streamline operations."* She forces a smile, her mind racing. *Will this "streamlining" cut members of her team?*

In a suburban kitchen, 58-year-old Sam sips coffee. He reads about AI-driven robots being used at a factory like the one he's worked in for thirty years. He hoped to ride his job into retirement, but now he isn't so sure. *Is there still a place for workers like me?*

Three people at three career stages face the same reality. The AI age isn't coming, it's here. And it's shaking up careers in real time.

What the Research Says

These stories reflect the massive workforce shifts underway. For years, experts warned about AI and automation upending job markets. Now, data confirms that it has. In 2023, surveyed employers projected a **23% job churn** (creation plus elimination) by 2027. If true, roughly a quarter of all US jobs will undergo disruption by 2027 (World Economic Forum [WEF], 2023).

Globally, 92 million jobs could disappear by 2030, with 170 million new ones being created. That's a net gain driven by tech and other trends (WEF, 2025). Many old roles will fade, but new roles (many not even invented) will fill the void (WEF, 2025). Not long ago, such disruption might have sounded far-fetched. Today it's a mainstream expectation.

To be clear, jobs aren't vanishing into a black hole without replacement. History shows technology creates new opportunities even as it destroys old ones. **Some 60% of workers have jobs that** *didn't exist* **in 1940** (Dizikes, 2024). Many modern jobs (from software developer to digital marketer) are "new work" that came out with new tech.

Over the long run, technology creates more jobs than it eliminates. Much of the past 80 years of employment growth has come from roles made possible by new technologies (Goldman Sachs, 2023). That's why experts say, *AI won't just take over work–it will also prompt new kinds of work*.

That's cold comfort if your *current* job feels at risk. Remember, most jobs will be only partly automated, at least at first. AI tends to **handle tasks, not entire occupations**. McKinsey found that fewer than 5% of jobs are entirely automatable with current technology. In some 60% of jobs, at least one-third of work tasks could be automated.

Most of us won't get a sudden pink slip from a robot. Instead, we'll see parts of our job change or phase out. Even if your title stays the same, the work you do is changing fast. Economists say that generative AI could expose **300 million jobs worldwide** to automation (Goldman Sachs, 2023).

Many global work tasks (up to one in five) could be done by AI in the near future (Goldman Sachs, 2023). It's not just factory or clerical work at stake. AI is stepping on creative and knowledge work once thought safe.

How AI prompts job losses is complicated. Historically, many jobs survive automation by *changing*. People refocus on tasks machines can't do well. Bank tellers didn't all lose their jobs to ATMs. Their day-to-day work shifted to relationship banking and complex customer service.

Likewise, today's customer service reps find that AI chatbots handle simple inquiries. Humans tackle more complicated cases. The job isn't gone, but it's changing fast. And fewer humans may eventually be needed.

In one study, 41% of surveyed employers planned to use AI to reduce human workforce (WEF, 2025) and about half of them expect AI to prompt job growth in other areas (WEF, 2023). The outlook is rapid turnover: jobs will shift, decline, grow, and evolve.

7-Step Survival Plan

This is not another tech-doomsday prophecy. It's a practical guide to help you take control of your career amid the AI upheaval.

The promise to you is straightforward. By the end of this journey, you will have a 7-step action plan grounded in essential human skills and strategies. This can keep you valuable and adaptable, however fast automation moves.

These seven steps work whether you're job-hunting, climbing the ladder, or trying to stay relevant in your current role. Here's a quick preview of our journey.

1. **Future-Proof Mindset.** *How to* cultivate mental flexibility and resilience in the face of rapid changes. A growth mindset and comfort with change are the new job security in the AI age.
2. **Upgrade Constantly.** *How to* embrace continuous learning and upskilling as a core habit. The best defense

against automation is *evolving* your skill set—always be a student of new tools, technologies, and in-demand human skills.

3. **AI + You.** *How to* leverage AI tools to work for you rather than against you. Learn to use AI in your job search and daily work. Turn these tools into value-enhancing allies.

4. **Work Smarter with AI.** *How to* integrate AI into your workflow. Mastering the art of prompting AI systems. Collaborate with AI on tasks. Avoid common pitfalls. Achieve more with less effort.

5. **Double Down on Human Skills.** *How to* hone your uniquely human abilities. Creative problem-solving, interpersonal communication, leadership, empathy. Machines can't replicate these well. Sharpen and showcase your skills. Stand out in AI-saturated workplaces.

6. **Build Your Brand and Network.** *How to* strengthen your professional network and personal brand in a digital world. Opportunities come from those who know you (and your skills). We'll cover networking tactics, online and offline, and ways to highlight your value.

7. **Career Agility.** *How to* embrace agility as the new normal. In a world of constant disruption, the ability to pivot is crucial. Shift role, industries, or even start something of your own. We'll explore how to spot new opportunities and reinvent yourself when needed. Ride the waves of change. Don't be drowned by them.

Each step gets its own chapter in Part II, packed with examples, research, and quick-start tips. Together, they form your career upgrade toolkit. This isn't about needing to become a coder or AI engineer (unless you want to). It's about doubling down on what makes you **irreplaceably human** in the workplace and learning to work *with* the machines, not against them.

Why This Matters Now

Let's address the elephant in the room. Why the urgency? Because *waiting* is riskier than acting. By many accounts, AI's rise is the biggest workforce shake-up since the internet. It's just happening much faster.

Consider AI's rapid spread.

It took over 50 years from the installation of the first centralized power station before electricity-powered factories were mainstream. After the internet was available to the public, it took some 10 years before it was mainstream.

AI is one of the most rapidly adopted technologies in history. For example, "ChatGPT, hit an unprecedented **100 million users in just two months** (Hu, 2023)."

In the corporate world, the pace of adoption is relentless. In a survey of over 1400 companies in 101 countries, 78% reported using AI in at least one business function (McKinsey, 2024). This is up from 55% in 2023– a big rise in adoption in just one year.

Most companies are exploring it in some form. Every year, more companies adopt AI solutions, handing more tasks to algorithms. If this feels fast, that's because it is. We are living through one of the fastest industrial revolutions to date.

AI is automating routine tasks and enhancing other tasks. It is making decisions that affect people's careers. "See how it all plays out" is not a safe strategy. By the time the picture is clear, you could be left behind.

Action beats anxiety. Small proactive steps can make a huge difference in where you stand a year or two from now. Learn a new digital skill, try an AI tool, or reach out to your network. As they say, the best time to adapt was yesterday, but the second-best time is today.

The silver lining is that now is also the best time to *seize new opportunities*. AI isn't just a threat. It's also creating entirely new markets and roles. Companies are hungry for people who can bridge human creativity with AI-driven efficiency.

The playing field is being reset. From recent grads to mid-career professionals, this is your chance to leapfrog others stuck in old ways. But only if you prepare yourself. This book will help you turn fear into focus, uncertainty into action.

Your career is not your job title. It's your skillset and mindset. Jobs may come and go. But the right skills, learning, and changes, will keep you relevant. As you read on, remember, be the driver of your career, not a passenger.

The AI disruption road is full of twists and bumps. This guide is a map and a shock absorber for your journey. The ride might be bumpy. But the right navigation tools can lead to new landscapes of opportunity.

> **Half of all work tasks could be automated by 2030.**
> McKinsey Global Institute (2017)

That projection sounds daunting, but it's not a death sentence. It's a wake-up call. The Great Disruption is here. It's time to gear up rather than give up.

Do This Now: Kickstart Your Adaptability

Take simple action now for stronger adaptability.

List at Least 3 Work Tasks

List tasks you perform regularly that could be fully or partially automated. (Think, monthly report compilation, sorting customer emails, scheduling meetings). Be honest with yourself. This personal 'task audit' reveals your exposure to automation.

Learn an AI Trend in Your Field

Learn something new about how AI is used in your industry this week. Do a quick search for 'AI in [Your Industry]' and read a recent article or report. If you're in marketing, explore AI tools for drafting social media posts. If you're in healthcare, read about AI assisting in triage. Knowledge is power. Staying informed can inspire ideas and reduce fear of the unknown.

Compare Notes With a Colleague

Reach out to a colleague or friend about how AI is changing their work. Swap observations. Share strategies. Starting this conversation can give you practical tips or resources. Plus, you're signaling your network that you're proactively engaged with this topic. Position yourself as a "go-to AI person" in your circle by being curious and open.

If you'd like printable worksheets to make these reflections easier, see the Bonus Extras at the end of Part I.

Chapter 2
The Automation Shockwave

AI isn't taking over jobs overnight. It's taking over *tasks*, bit by bit. This is the first reality to grasp as the automation shockwave sweeps through work as we know it.

Picture a typical day at your job and break it into tasks—answering emails, analyzing spreadsheets, greeting clients, writing reports.

AI excels at automating specific tasks, especially routine, repeatable ones. That's how disruption often starts: not with mass layoffs, but with parts of your work quietly evaporating.

Tasks Before Jobs: The First Wave of Change

Consider Jenna, a mid-level accountant. Ten years ago, she spent hours cross-checking invoices and inputting data. Today, her company's AI-driven software automatically tallies receipts and flags anomalies in seconds. Jenna is still employed, but her role has evolved. She focuses on interpreting software's reports and advising clients.

Data-entry tasks that used to consume her time are largely done by algorithms. We've seen this pattern before. In the 1970s, bank tellers feared ATMs would erase their jobs. ATMs did take over routine cash-handling tasks, yet bank tellers shifted to new tasks like customer service and sales. Jobs survived through *task transformation*.

Research backs this up. Few occupations are fully automatable with current technology. One study put the number at under 5%. However, in about 60% of jobs, at least 30% of the tasks could be done by machines. A significant portion of your tasks might eventually be handled by AI or robotics, even if your job isn't completely "robot-proof".

Recent analysis of AI capabilities echoes this. Some two-thirds of jobs include tasks AI could perform, with **25% to 50%** of the work **potentially automatable** (Goldman Sachs, 2023)—a huge chunk.

Imagine an average workweek where one or two days' worth of your tasks are handled by an AI. That's the scale of change we're talking about.

What does this mean for you? It means partial automation is already underway. You might not lose your job title.

But the work could become very different. If you're a project manager who spends time drafting status updates, an AI tool can draft them for you. If you're a nurse who spends evenings inputting patient notes, an AI assistant can transcribe and pre-fill reports.

These tools are introduced as "help." And they are helpful. But there's a flip side. When tasks get automated, jobs get redefined. Maybe your team won't need five people doing the same tasks once AI steps in.

Task-by-task encroachment is how automation begins, often under the radar. One day you realize that your role looks very different than it used to.

How Fast Is It Coming?

The big question is, "How fast will this all happen?" Faster than previous disruptions, but not all at once, though technology adoption is accelerating at unprecedented rates.

It took over 50 years for electricity to become commonplace in industry after the first commercial power station was introduced in the late 1800s. It took the internet about 10 years after its introduction to the public before it reached most of the world population of approximately 8 billion.

AI reportedly gained nearly 2 billion users worldwide in its first two years, an unprecedented uptake (Carolan et al., 2025). When a breakthrough capability like AI arrives, it can be everywhere in a blink.

In the business and personal world, AI adoption is also moving at rocket speed. In 2023, roughly 55% of surveyed organizations used AI in at least one function (McKinsey, 2024). By 2024, that jumped to **78%**.

Most companies are exploring AI, even if just in pilot projects. The McKinsey report predicts that by 2030 some 70% of companies will adopt AI technologies in some form.

The adoption curve isn't a gentle slope; it's a steep climb.

That said, "adoption" doesn't always mean full integration. Often, initial adoption is shallow. A company might implement one AI tool or run a small pilot. There's usually a lag between early experiments and widespread, deep integration across all workflows. This is where timelines can stretch out a bit.

Take autonomous vehicles. A few years ago, hype suggested self-driving cars would be everywhere by now. The progress is real. Some cities have robo-taxis, and many cars have autopilot features. But fully driverless cars without human safety nets are *still* not mainstream in 2025.

Many industries follow this pattern. First there's a burst of hype and trial deployments. Then there are years of improvements and overcoming practical hurdles before the technology is truly mainstream.

Think of it as two curves. The **hype curve** shoots up almost vertically. That represents excitement and early adoption. The **deployment curve** is more gradual. That's the longer slog of integrating tech into every corner of business operations.

AI is now at peak hype, in a rapid trial phase. But broad and deep deployment is ongoing and will continue for several years. By most estimates, the steepest AI deployment curve in many sectors will hit in the latter half of this decade. By 2030 half of work tasks in many industries could be automated in some way, given current trends (WEF, 2023).

AI came with striking forecasts. Gartner predicted that by 2025, most phone and online customer service interactions would involve AI (as cited in *The Future of Commerce*, 2024). Similarly, tech firm Servion predicted that **95%** of phone or internet **customer interactions** would be handled by AI by 2025 (Lauder, 2025). Reality is more modest–perhaps 20–30%, mostly via basic chatbots. But it's increasing every year.

In manufacturing, **robot density** (robots per 10,000 workers) in factories worldwide doubled between 2015 and 2023 (IFR, 2024), enabling faster production with fewer manual labor hours. In Amazon's warehouses, over **520,000 robotic drive units** move goods alongside human workers (Amazon, n.d.). And that number is climbing. Such stats indicate a concentrated wave of adoption *now*, not in some distant future.

The 2020s are truly the decade of AI and automation rollout.

If all this feels head-spinning fast, that's because it is. But fast adoption doesn't mean instant, across-the-board transformation. The effects will arrive sooner in some fields (routine office work, customer service, data processing) and later in others (complex manual trades, jobs requiring high social intelligence).

Nonetheless, the trajectory is clear. Every year, more organizations will be flipping the switch on AI solutions. Every year, more tasks will be handed off to algorithms or robots. The time to prepare is not when the change is "over." It's *now, while it's unfolding*.

Separating Hype from Reality

With all this rapid change, it's crucial to distinguish myth from reality. On social media (and sometimes in boardrooms), you hear extreme statements. *"AI will replace everyone in two years!"* or, *"AI will create a utopia where no one needs to work."*

Neither is true. Reality is more nuanced. Yes, AI is advancing fast—faster than many expected. But there are limits to what today's AI can do and many barriers to full automation.

In early 2023 there was a wave of panic that AI like ChatGPT would instantly replace jobs in writing, programming, design, etc. What's really happening? AI can indeed produce content. But often it's draft quality that needs a human touch.

A large marketing firm might use AI to generate first-draft social media posts or simple product descriptions—reducing some repetitive writing work. But that doesn't mean it fires all its copywriters. Instead, maybe each writer now manages more content, with AI doing 50% of the initial grunt work.

Similarly, AI might generate code snippets for a software engineer. But the engineer then integrates and fixes that code. The job shifts towards more oversight and quality control. Far from "no humans needed," we see **collaboration models** emerging in many areas. AI produces output, humans curate and refine it.

Another reality check. Even when AI *can* do something in theory, organizations often won't implement it immediately (or properly). There are cost issues, integration challenges, and trust factors.

A company might test an AI tool and find that it saves time but makes subtle errors. So, they hold off widespread use until it improves. Or employees resist correct usage, limiting impact. Human and organizational elements slow the theoretical pace of change.

On the other hand, don't dismiss the tech. Some skeptics in the 2010s said, "AI will never drive cars" or "AI can't be creative." Those views look outdated now. The better stance is a balanced one.

Be a realist.

Don't buy into doomsday prophecies that AI will leave everyone jobless in a blink. Mass unemployment is *not* imminent. And historically, technology creates jobs and displaces them.

But don't fall for complacency. AI is steadily growing more capable and handling more tasks. The impact on jobs is **cumulative** and accelerating, even if the most dire predictions were overhyped.

Companies have slightly **revised down** their short-term automation expectations compared to a few years ago. In 2020, surveyed business leaders thought 47% of tasks would be automated by 2025. Now the consensus is 42% by 2027 (WEF, 2023).

A bit less aggressive, but it's still a massive shift. And surprise leaps can happen. The rise of ChatGPT, the first publicly available AI chatbot, in late 2022 caught many off guard. Suddenly it was possible for AI to tackle previously untouchable creative and knowledge work (like writing and coding).

Separating hype from reality means staying grounded. AI won't replace all workers in a year or two. But it will change how almost everyone works over the next decade. Not every flashy demo will translate into an overnight revolution. But enough of them will that you can't ignore this trend.

Think of AI neither as magic nor fad but as a powerful new set of tools—tools that are steadily being adopted, tool by tool, task by task.

Impact Across Industries

The AI shockwave is not hitting all industries evenly. Let's tour a few sectors to see what's really changing on the ground.

Manufacturing & Warehousing

Robots have been on factory floors for decades. Now AI is giving them vision and "brains." Today's industrial robots can learn and adapt rather than mindlessly repeat motions. The global average robot density in factories reached 162 per 10,000 workers in 2023—more than double what it was just seven years prior (IFR, 2024).

Likewise, many factories have twice as many robots per worker than they did in the mid-2010s. In Amazon's fulfillment centers, over 520,000 autonomous robots scurry around moving goods and handling heavy lifting and fetching. Meanwhile, human workers pack and supervise (Amazon, n.d.).

Warehouses ship packages faster and more cost effectively and need fewer people for repetitive labor. They now hire more robot technicians and maintenance staff—a shift in the type of jobs available. The work is still there. But it's gradually tilting from pure manual labor to tech-supported roles.

Customer Service & Retail

If you've called a support line or chatted with an online help agent recently, you've likely interacted with AI. Simple, common queries are often handled by chatbots or automated phone systems. ("Where is my order?" "Reset my password.")

Many companies have trimmed call-center staff or shifted them to only complex calls. In retail stores and fast-food restaurants, self-service kiosks and AI-driven voice ordering are becoming common. Fewer cashiers are needed when customers can check out or place orders via a screen or app.

Remaining roles tend to focus on higher-touch services: handling exceptions, personalized assistance, upselling, and customer relationships. **Frontline service jobs** are evolving, not disappearing outright. A cashier might evolve to a customer experience associate. Undeniably, fewer people are required for routine transactions.

Healthcare

This field shows the breadth of AI's promise.

Algorithms read medical images (X-rays, MRIs) with impressive accuracy—sometimes nearly on par with radiologists for certain types of diagnoses (McKinney et al., 2020). AI can listen to patients' symptoms and suggest possible conditions, functioning like an advanced diagnostic aid (Blease et al., 2019). During the COVID-19 pandemic, hospitals used AI models to predict patient surges and manage resources (Wynants et al., 2020).

These tools haven't replaced doctors. They *assist* them. A radiologist with AI might catch subtle details more reliably. But humans still confirm diagnoses and communicate with patients. In telemedicine, AI chat assistants gather initial info ("virtual intake"). But a nurse or doctor takes over.

Consider nursing tasks: lifting patients, perceiving mood changes, offering empathy. Those remain **hands-on and deeply human**. You can't automate empathetic bedside manner or dexterity for inserting an IV (at least not yet).

Healthcare is seeing more *collaborative models*. AI does number crunching and pattern recognition. Humans do empathy, complex decision-making, moral judgment, and personal touch.

Finance & Law

Banks have used AI for years in certain niches—like detecting fraudulent transactions in real time (something no team of humans could match across millions of transactions). Automated trading algorithms transformed stock markets long ago. Now, AI "robo-advisors" manage investment portfolios for consumers at low fees, threatening the roles of financial advisors who only perform basic portfolio rebalancing.

In law, AI can sift through thousands of discovery documents or a first draft of a simple contract. What used to take junior lawyers or paralegals weeks can be done in hours with AI software. Fewer entry-level attorneys are needed for document review grunt work.

Higher-level work–advising clients, negotiating deals, appearing in court–remains human for now. AI is also enabling *new* services. Some smaller law firms use AI to handle tasks they previously couldn't afford to do, letting them serve more clients or take on more cases.

The net effect is a productivity boost but also a shift in required skills (lawyers with data and tech literacy are in higher demand). In finance, while AI automates clerical tasks, it also opens roles in fintech, data analysis, and AI oversight/regulation.

Education

AI tutoring systems can provide practice exercises and feedback to students in most subjects. They aren't replacing teachers, but they are changing the teacher's role. Instead of lecturing uniformly to 30 students, AI tools can help personalize practice for each student.

Let AI software handle multiplication tables or verb conjugation drills, while teachers focus on one-on-one coaching, mentoring, and motivating students. Administrative tasks like grading multiple-choice quizzes are automated in many schools, freeing teachers for lesson planning and individual help. AI tools can help evaluate student essays or suggest lesson plan outlines.

On the upside, teachers save time on rote tasks. The downside or challenge: teachers need *new skills* to effectively integrate these tools and double-check AI's outputs for accuracy and bias.

The education industry hasn't been upended as dramatically as some. But it's gradually shifting toward a model where AI handles routine instruction and assessment, and humans focus on mentorship and creative teaching.

What These Industry Shifts Mean for You

Across these examples, the pattern is clear. **AI is great at narrow tasks** that when strung together can reshape jobs.

- **Factories** still have workers. But technicians now outweigh assembly line laborers.
- **Call Centers** still employ humans. But they deal with escalated issues, not password resets.
- **Banks** still have analysts. But they use AI-generated insights to make decisions, instead of manually crunching numbers for days.

It's critical to note: AI is *creating* new roles and even new industries. Entire job categories barely existed a few years ago: **data scientist, AI model trainer, prompt engineer, AI ethicist.**

- **Cybersecurity** is booming, partly because AI enables new cyber threats. And skilled professionals are needed to counteract them.

- **E-commerce** is exploding with algorithms optimizing logistics, creating roles in digital supply chain management and warehouse automation supervision.

If you can spot *where* AI is in use in an industry, you can spot emerging needs and jobs:

- **Healthcare**: Hospitals use AI for data analysis, healthcare data analysts and AI system integrators in clinical settings will be in demand.

- **Design**: Graphic designers using AI image generators will create niches for "AI art curators" and specialists who draw creative outcomes from those tools.

The AI shockwave is uneven but wide-reaching. No industry is completely untouched. But the timeline and nature of change vary sector by sector. The exercises below can keep you informed about what's happening in *your* field, so you'll be ready to pivot as tasks evolve.

Do This Now: Adapt to AI's Impact

Concrete steps to understand and adapt to AI's impact in your industry.

Map Your Tasks

Write down your main tasks at work. Mark them as High, Medium, or Low for AI takeover potential. *High* = routine, rules-based, or data-heavy (an algorithm could handle it soon). *Low* = tasks requiring human touch, judgment, or creativity that AI can't do well. This personal "task exposure audit" will spotlight where you're most vulnerable.

Research Your Industry

Find one recent report or credible article on AI use in your line of work. If you're in marketing, look up AI in ad targeting. If you're in finance, search for AI in risk analysis. Knowing the latest industry trends and timelines gives you a competitive edge. Soon, you'll be among the first to spot coming changes.

Try an AI Tool

Identify one AI-powered tool relevant to your work and spend an hour experimenting with it. In sales? Try a CRM plugin that uses AI to forecast leads. A writer? Try an AI text generator for outlines.

Hands-on experience will demystify AI and replace fear with familiarity. You don't have to become an expert overnight. Just dip your toes in.

Start the Conversation at Work

Bring up AI in your next team meeting or one-on-one with your manager. Ask if the company is exploring new automation or AI projects. Express your interest in being involved or piloting new tools.

This positions you as proactive rather than reactive. If layoffs or role changes are coming, try to be on the side driving the change (or at least aware of it). Don't get caught off guard.

Stay Skeptical and Curious

Commit to investigating one hyped claim about AI. If an article says "AI can replace X job entirely," do a bit of digging. Is it realistic or a catchy headline? Likewise, if someone claims "AI could never do Y," check the current research. Training yourself to separate buzz from facts will help you maintain a clear head amid the noise.

> **Companion worksheets are available to guide this exercise—check the Bonus Extras at the end of Part I.**

Each small action you take now is an investment in your adaptability. You'll buffer yourself against the shockwave's negative effects. And you'll see *opportunities* hidden in the disruption.

Next chapter, dive deeper into those opportunities. Examine the new "rules" of work. Learn which roles are most at risk from AI, and which are more secure. Learn to map your own career onto that spectrum and keep the momentum going.

Chapter 3
The New Rules of Work

Not all jobs face AI disruption equally. Some roles are in the bullseye of automation. Others are relatively shielded by their very nature. To see where you stand, you need to understand **task exposure**. Look at *day-to-day* tasks rather than job titles. Here, we'll view roles more vulnerable to automation and roles more resilient. We'll also walk through role-mapping exercises to help you pivot from vulnerable to resilient in your career.

The Task Exposure Lens:
Why the Same Job Can Be Safe or Risky

Jobs are essentially bundles of tasks. The key question isn't *"Will AI take my job?"* but **"Can AI do my job?"** The more of your tasks AI can handle, the more *exposed* your role is to disruption.

Consider an administrative assistant. Their task list might include scheduling meetings, data entry, formatting documents, and greeting clients. Scheduling and data entry are highly automatable. Algorithms can manage calendars and software auto fills data. Formatting documents can be semi-automated with templates and macros.

But greeting clients and handling unexpected requests? Those still need a human touch. An admin assistant's job could be 60% automatable tasks and 40% human-centric tasks. That role is ***quite exposed***. Over half of it could, in theory, be done by software.

Contrast that with a kindergarten teacher. Key tasks: keeping a room of 5-year-olds safe and engaged, teaching basic skills, managing conflicts, communicating with parents. Most of that requires human empathy, quick judgment, and physical presence.

AI might help with lesson plan ideas or educational apps for drills. But core tasks, maintaining order in a lively classroom and nurturing children, are not currently automatable. A teacher's task exposure might be 10-20%. The teacher role is **more resilient** by nature.

Studies have tried to quantify this across occupations, finding certain job categories had greater exposure than others. Generally, roles involving routine information processing showed high automation potential. Think clerical work, basic accounting, assembly-line manufacturing. Jobs requiring high social and creative work and unpredictable physical work showed less risk.

Another recent study on AI's latest wave found that some high-skill jobs include many tasks that AI can do. Financial analysts can spend hours building forecast models in Excel. AI can automate chunks of that modeling work. A translator's core task is converting text from one language to another. AI can do it instantly with surprising accuracy.

Exposure isn't purely low-skill vs. high-skill; it's task by task. A chief executive likely has low exposure because their tasks involve strategy, ambiguous problem-solving, and people management. An entry-level accountant has higher exposure. Their tasks involve data processing and rule-based decision-making, which AI excels at.

Think of task exposure as your job's "automation risk percentage."

That's a sign to transition to a healthier role—either within your current job or in a new one. If 70% of your role is made up of tasks that are easy for AI to do, you should actively carve a new niche for yourself—either in your current job or in another.

If your exposure is low, don't get complacent. Few jobs are fully automation proof. Even therapists use AI tools for cognitive behavioral therapy exercises. But you have a cushion to adapt gradually.

10 At-Risk Job Categories

Below are **10 At-Risk Job Categories** in the age of AI, along with why they're vulnerable. These aren't the only jobs that will change, but they highlight the kinds of roles most exposed to automation.

Customer Service Representatives

Handling routine inquiries is a big part of this job. And AI chatbots and voice agents are increasingly good at it.

Simple requests like order tracking, password resets, or FAQs can often be resolved without humans. As natural language AI improves, even moderately complex queries can be handled by machines. Fewer live agents are needed for the same volume of customer interactions.

Fact bomb: One tech firm predicted that by 2025, **95% of customer interactions would be AI powered**, illustrating the pressure on this role (Lauder, 2017).

Current levels are lower, but the trend is clear. Human reps won't disappear. The remaining ones will handle the hardest problems and customers. It will likely require higher-level skills (and emotional resilience). And fewer traditional call center positions will exist.

Data Entry Clerks / Administrative Assistants

These roles revolve around structured, repetitive tasks—the sweet spot for software automation.

Modern OCR (optical character recognition) can digitize and enter form data faster and more accurately than people. Scheduling tools like Calendly automate meeting coordination. Routine emails or documents can be drafted by templates or simple AI.

We're already seeing these roles decline. One executive assistant often does what a team of assistants did a decade ago, thanks to digital tools.

"Data Entry Clerk" is one of the fastest-declining job titles as companies adopt AI and software for those functions (WEF, 2025).

Core administrative support jobs are shrinking. Those remaining are often rebranded as office manager or project coordinator positions. The focus is on human elements software can't do (yet).

Translators and Interpreters

AI translation has improved drastically.

With apps like Google Translate and DeepL, and devices that interpret speech in real-time, large chunks of everyday translation needs can be handled by machines.

Microsoft researchers note that "Interpreters and Translators" are among the jobs most **suited to AI tools**. Nearly all their routine work can be replicated by current AI models (Soper, 2025).

To be fair, truly **nuanced** translation (literary translation, sensitive diplomatic interpreting) still benefits from human skill. But for many businesses and travelers, AI makes basic translation a solved problem.

This isn't the end of translation jobs. But it drastically reduces the demand for human translators for basic documents or standard conversations. Human translators may shift to post-editing AI translations or handling only specialized texts.

Writers and Content Creators (for Routine Content)

If your job is to produce formulaic or boilerplate text, AI is encroaching fast.

AI can draft news briefs (provide sports scores, weather reports), basic marketing copy, product descriptions, and code. Some media outlets use AI to generate short company earnings reports or sports game recaps, repetitive formats where plugging data into a narrative template works well.

A creative copywriter brainstorming a brand campaign is safer (AI isn't creative or strategic in the human sense). But a junior content writer churning out 20 SEO-friendly blog posts a week is at risk. We've also seen AI used for first drafts of press releases or routine legal contracts that humans refine.

The key distinction is **original creative insight** vs. formulaic writing. Jobs heavy on the latter are vulnerable. Going forward, writers might find their role shifting to editor/curator. They'll review and polish AI-generated drafts, not write from scratch.

Sales and Telemarketing

For roles like telemarketer or entry-level sales development reps, AI can handle initial outreach at scale. Think automated emails and LinkedIn messages, qualifying leads on a website, even cold calling from a script. One person with an AI assistant now does the work of a room of telemarketers.

AI-driven sales tools can send personalized intro emails to thousands of prospects and triage the responses. A human rep only engages when a lead is promising and ready for a human conversation.

Telemarketing and sales roles with scripted pitches **are highly automatable and extremely vulnerable**. High-level sales (enterprise sales, consultative selling) where relationships and complex negotiations matter remain in human hands.

Expect fewer junior sales call-dialers, and more human "closers" who build trust and handle complexity—potentially leveraging AI for prep work.

Bookkeeping and Accounting Clerks

These roles involve applying set rules to numbers—recording transactions, reconciling accounts, calculating payroll, preparing financial statements.

Software like QuickBooks and FreshBooks already automates much small-business bookkeeping. AI can classify expenses, detect anomalies, and suggest journal entries. Clerical accounting work is being swallowed by algorithms, reducing the need for large teams of junior accountants.

Clearly, strategic finance and complex tax planning still need human expertise. But the days of entry-level accountants manually inputting and checking thousands of entries are fading.

The U.S. Bureau of Labor Statistics projects declines in bookkeeping clerk positions this decade, aligning with these trends. Accounting professionals who thrive will move up in the value chain. They'll focus on analysis, advising, and ensuring AI outputs make sense.

Manufacturing Assembly Line Workers / Machine Operators

In predictable environments, factory automation isn't new. But AI and advanced robotics are expanding automatable tasks.

Roles like assembly worker, pick-and-place machine operator, and welder in highly structured settings (like automotive manufacturing plants) have been increasingly taken over by robots.

Computer numerical control (CNC) machine operator/programmer, a related role, may be highly automatable. AI can learn patterns to control machining processes. It can even generate code for cutting parts.

In warehouses, jobs involving driving forklifts or sorting items are being replaced by self-driving machines and conveyor systems guided by AI vision. The common theme is repetitive physical work in a controlled environment. Each year, the balance shifts more toward machines on the factory floor.

However, it's worth noting that humans are still needed for maintenance, troubleshooting, and tasks requiring flexibility and fine dexterity. Those are tasks robots haven't mastered. We also see new manufacturing jobs emerging around managing automation (robot maintenance techs, automation supervisors).

Retail Cashiers and Clerks

If you've used a self-checkout kiosk at or seen Amazon's experimental "Just Walk Out" stores (sensors and AI charge you as you leave), you understand the trend.

Routine retail transactions are primed for automation. With self-checkout systems and payment apps, we need fewer clerks. Inventory tracking with smart sensors also reduces the need for clerks. **Online shopping**, built on AI recommendation engines and automated fulfillment, limits demand for in-store retail roles.

The roles that remain in retail are shifting toward customer experience–personal shoppers, product experts, or handling in-person services. But traditional cashier jobs involving scanning items and taking payments will likely keep shrinking.

For perspective, it was predicted that by the mid-2020s, over 80% of retail transactions in stores would be automated. We're not universally there yet. But many chains are moving toward that.

Entry-Level Analysts and Researchers

For junior roles in data analysis, insurance underwriting, and basic research support, the risk of automation is significant. Jobs that center on gathering information, compiling reports, or doing formulaic analysis are especially vulnerable.

AI crunches datasets, summarizes, and identifies patterns far faster than humans. It can scan thousands of insurance claims and flag those that look fraudulent in minutes. This task used to keep teams of claims analysts busy. AI can take a year of sales data and generate a report of key insights.

High-level judgment still needs people. This includes deciding on strategies based on data and understanding why something happened. But many support roles–the junior analyst churning out Excel reports, the market researcher pulling info for a slide deck. These may be augmented by AI or made redundant if AI tools are directly usable by decision-makers.

Upskilling is the path here. Those in analytical roles need to move toward interpretation, communication, and domain expertise, not just number-crunching.

Secretaries and Receptionists

Automated phone systems and digital assistants handle more tasks that traditional secretaries and receptionists once did.

Voice menus route calls and chatbots answer common questions—a role once handled by office receptionists. Calendar apps schedule meetings that executive's secretaries used to coordinate. Electronic visitor kiosks in lobbies register guests and notify employees without human gatekeepers.

We aren't yet at the point where every front desk is unstaffed. Many orgs value the human touch for greeting visitors or handling complex scheduling. But far less staff are needed. One person often manages tasks a team of admins did in the past.

These roles are evolving towards office management, event planning, and other duties needing human coordination and decision-making. Many traditional "typing and answering phones" secretary jobs have been absorbed by technology with the work redistributed.

What These Industry Shifts Mean for You

If you didn't see your exact job title in the list above, focus on the *nature* of the work. Ask yourself:

- Is it repetitive?
- Rules-based?
- Heavily data-oriented?
- Largely done on a computer?

If yes to many of these, your role may have higher exposure.

If your work is customer-facing, unpredictable, or hands-on, it has lower exposure. The new rule of thumb? What you do matters more than your title. Even within the same profession, two people can have different exposures.

A software developer maintaining routine code is more automatable than a software engineer designing system architecture. Yet both are considered "software engineer" jobs. A teaching job running drills is more automatable than one centered on mentoring students.

Top 10 Resilient Job Categories

The good news is certain roles are *relatively* resilient to AI. Let's look at **Top 10 Resilient Job Categories** and why they're safer (for now).

Healthcare & Personal Care Workers

Nurses, Nursing Aides, Caregivers, Doctors, Surgeons

These roles require physical presence, complex human empathy, and on-the-spot adaptability.

A nursing assistant might lift and reposition patients, notice subtle changes in a patient's mood or condition, or comfort someone in pain. These are difficult for robots or AI to do in real, uncontrolled environments like hospitals.

As populations age, demand for these roles is increasing. And technology is augmenting rather than replacing them. Yes, there are medical robots. But they typically handle specific tasks (like delivering supplies around a hospital) and assist human staff.

The core of nursing and caregiving—direct human-to-human care—remains firmly in human hands. Nursing and care roles rank among those least likely to be upended by AI, according to multiple reports. These jobs are safe because of the technical challenges of automation and because they involve trust, compassion, and judgment, which we expect from people, not machines.

Healthcare specialists such as doctors and surgeons are also relatively resilient. While AI is making waves by diagnosing from images and suggesting treatments from big data, medicine is as much art as science. Surgeons performing intricate procedures and doctors developing complex treatment plans rely on human judgment, ethics, and responsibility that machines lack. Tools like robotic surgery extend human capability but remain under direct human control.

Some GP tasks are increasingly assisted by AI, but the role remains human-led when it comes to judgment and patient trust.

Teachers and Educators

Teaching involves complex human interaction. AI tutors can help students practice math problems. But inspiring students, managing classrooms, and understanding why Johnny is acting out require human insight.

Social and emotional skills are teachers' forte and are not automatable. Teachers who use AI tools to offload grading or provide adaptive practice for students will have an easier time. Those who don't adapt might struggle.

But the core job of teaching—understanding each student's needs, fostering critical thinking, motivating kids—stays in human hands. Be it pre-school, higher education, or corporate training, similar logic applies. Mentors and coaches who guide learning journeys aren't getting replaced by AI, but they may change how they teach.

We will likely always want humans in education because it's fundamentally a people development process. Also, society is not keen to hand over children's education entirely to machines. There's a trust and accountability factor.

Social Workers, Therapists, Psychologists

These are centered on human connection, empathy, and understanding nuanced personal situations.

Could an AI chatbot counsel someone? To a limited extent, yes. Some mental health apps use AI for cognitive-behavioral therapy exercises and as a non-judgmental ear. But for deep emotional issues, trauma, relationship counseling, etc., most people want a human who can truly *listen* and *care*.

Therapy involves building trust over time, reading between the lines of what's said (and not said), and tailoring approaches to an individual's evolving needs. AI lacks genuine empathy and moral judgment. It can't fully grasp the uniqueness of a person's life story or the societal context of their issues.

Also, there's an element of accountability and ethics. If an AI gives bad mental health advice, who is responsible? For now, these roles are safe. Demand for them is rising in many regions because of increased mental health awareness. Social work often involves field visits, understanding community dynamics, and creative problem-solving for families. These are out of AI's realm.

Skilled Tradespeople

Electricians, Plumbers, Carpenters

Jobs in unpredictable physical environments requiring hands-on problem solving are hard to automate.

An electrician crawls through a century-old building's crawlspace to rewire it, or a plumber improvises a fix for a weirdly clogged pipe. Robots aren't doing that any time soon.

These trades require **dexterity, creativity, and on-site decision-making**. Each job site is different. Older structures and custom projects present distinct challenges. While tradespeople use tools and software, execution is set within the real world's chaos.

Robots struggle with that level of adaptability. These roles also often require certifications and dealing with safety issues. A mistake can mean a fire or flood. So, oversight is crucial.

Instead of replacing tradespeople, technology usually supports them. Augmented reality goggles can show pipe layouts behind walls. Power tools now offer smart assistance. In these cases, tech empowers human workers rather than taking their place.

Historically, automation in these fields tends toward enhanced tools (power saws, pipe cameras), not robot workers.

Jobs Requiring High Physical Interaction or Unpredictable Environments

Emergency Services, Security, Cleaning in Complex Settings

Roles like firefighter, emergency medical technician (EMT), police officer, and security officer deal with chaotic real-world scenarios.

In an emergency, such as a burning building, natural disaster, crime in progress, you need humans making split-second decisions with moral and practical judgment. Drones and AI may assist, ike surveying a fire or predicting crime hotspots. But on-the-ground responders will remain human indefinitely.

These jobs involve physical ability, comforting people in distress, making judgment calls under pressure, and adapting to whatever is happening. Likewise, cleaning or maintenance in non-standard environments remain human domains. Robots excel in structured environments like a flat factory floor. But put them in Grandma's antique-filled, unevenly floored house, and they're lost.

As a rule, **unstructured environments + need for improvisation = human job security**.

Another example. "Security guards" might seem automatable with cameras and AI. But many places still want a human presence for judgment and response. And human guards present greater deterrents than mere cameras.

Engineers and Maintenance Technicians

It may sound counterintuitive, since engineers work with technology, but many engineering roles are resilient. This is because they involve designing solutions for novel problems and overseeing complex systems.

The **creative problem-solving** many engineers do—whether designing a unique bridge or figuring out why a machine is malfunctioning—isn't something AI can fully handle. These tasks often require understanding context, running real-world tests, and iterative thinking.

Technicians who maintain industrial machines or infrastructure are also in demand. Machines can signal error (predictive maintenance sensors can alert technicians to an issue). But humans typically diagnose and fix the problems.

Also, as we deploy more robots and AI, humans install, repair, and update those systems. Robots don't yet maintain other robots autonomously. Roles focusing on *maintaining and improving* technology remain safe.

As a saying goes in IT: "AI won't take your job, but someone who knows AI might." Similarly, "Robots won't replace maintenance workers, but workers who can work with robots will replace those who can't."

Creative Professions

Artists, Designers, Creative Directors

AI can now generate images, whole novels, music, design layouts, and much more.

So, you might think creatives are doomed. But remember, **human creativity is more than making an image or sound**.

It's about context, emotion, storytelling, cultural relevance. A creative director at an ad agency isn't just churning out pictures. They're crafting campaigns that resonates with people. AI can quickly produce 100 variations of a concept. But deciding which concepts should be explored—and why they will connect with audiences—is a human strength.

We are seeing some AI impact. Graphic designers, for example, now use AI as a tool (speeding up generating concepts or tedious editing). This might reduce the need for some production-level design work. But new roles are also popping up, like "prompt designers" skilled at getting the best output from AI art generators.

The creative sector historically adapts by incorporating new tools rather than being replaced wholesale. Humans crave human stories and original perspectives. While AI can mimic style, it's remixing what it's seen. It doesn't *feel* or *truly understand*.

Jobs revolving around human creativity and innovation (including writers of original content, filmmakers, product designers) have resilience. They might use AI-based tools as productivity boosters, not total work replacements.

The *tools* change, but the essence of creative jobs—creating something meaningfully new—remains hard for AI alone.

Managers and Strategic Roles

Leadership and management positions involving strategizing, mentoring teams, negotiating, and making judgment calls when the future is unclear. Roles like this tend to be more resilient.

Managers might use AI analytics to inform decisions. For example, tools can gauge team sentiment or predict project risks. But deciding how to handle delicate team conflicts or which strategic directions to pursue requires human judgment.

Managing people requires emotional intelligence—motivating different personalities, mediating conflicts, understanding unwritten workplace dynamics. AI doesn't handle office politics or inspire teams with vision. The higher up the decision chain you go, the less automatable the roles. It becomes more about complex decision-making with incomplete data and taking on greater responsibility.

That said, managers will need to adapt, leveraging AI for data-driven decisions. The *nature* of management will evolve. Expect managers to oversee AI-augmented teams, interpret AI-generated insights, etc. But the roles themselves remain or become more crucial. Leaders who effectively marry human talent with AI capabilities will be in high demand.

Emerging Tech and AI Specialists

Obviously, people who develop or work *on* AI are in a good spot.

AI engineers, machine learning researchers, and data scientists are booming. These roles require creativity, deep technical expertise, and constant learning as the field advances.

Roles like AI ethicists, AI project managers, and robotics specialists are relatively safe. They are expanding AI capability and managing implementation. They ride the wave instead of getting hit by it. Tech jobs are at comparatively *lower* risk of automation. Ironically, it's because they involve designing and managing the automation (Goldman Sachs, 2023).

Even in tech, tasks can be automated. AI helps write code, but it doesn't replace developers. The takeaway? If you shift into new technologies, you're moving with progress, not against it. Talent shortages in these fields also make them less at risk of automation.

Entrepreneurship and Small Business Owners

Entrepreneurs and small business owners are among the most resilient roles in the age of AI. By definition, entrepreneurship involves creating new value, adapting to shifting markets, and taking risks. These are traits that no algorithm can replicate.

AI may empower entrepreneurs with tools for marketing, operations, and product development, but it won't replace their judgment, vision, or capacity for innovation. Starting and running a business requires spotting opportunities, connecting with customers, and making tough calls when conditions change. These are inherently human strengths.

Research often cites entrepreneurship as one of the least "automatable" career paths because it thrives on uncertainty and creativity. While AI can provide data and streamline tasks, it can't shoulder the responsibility of leadership, nor can it generate the conviction and persistence required to bring an idea to life.

The entrepreneurs who embrace AI as an ally—using it to reduce costs, test ideas, or reach customers faster—will thrive. Those who resist may find themselves disadvantaged. But the role itself, centered on human creativity and initiative, remains secure. In fact, AI may lower barriers to entry, enabling more people to become entrepreneurs by making once-costly tools affordable and accessible.

Traits of Resilient Roles

Jobs that are "safe" from AI (for now) share some traits. They call for social intelligence, like caring, negotiating, and building relationships. They also rely on creativity, innovation, physical dexterity, and adaptability—qualities machines can't match. These jobs often involve unpredictable scenarios or open-ended problem solving.

But a big caveat—*resilient doesn't mean static*. Being in a currently resilient role isn't a free pass to ignore AI.

Examples:

- **The best nurses will use AI tools for diagnostics or patient monitoring.**
- **The best teachers will use education tech to enhance learning, etc.**
- **The best professionals in human-heavy fields adopt AI to boost their performance.**

Those who use *AI tools* will outperform those who don't, even in human-heavy fields.

And some roles we think of as resilient could become less so over time as technology improves. Warehouse workers once seemed resilient due to the need for dexterity. But each year robots get a bit better at handling objects. We might say these roles are safe *for now*, with an eye on what could change in another decade.

The takeaway is: if your job is largely about **human strengths**—empathy, complexity, creativity, responsibility—

you're in a good place. Just be sure you continue to hone those strengths. Is your job largely about following established procedures with data or repetitive motions? Then you should be planning some moves.

Role-Mapping Pivot Exercise: Find Your Path to Resilience

It's time to put this into practice. Do a quick **role-mapping exercise** to identify vulnerable aspects of your current role and sketch out a path to more resilient footing. Grab a notebook or open a blank document.

STEP 1

Write your **job title** in the center of the page. Around it list 5-10 main tasks or responsibilities. Be specific.

If you're a marketing specialist, you might list:

- Write social media posts
- Run ad performance reports
- Brainstorm campaign ideas
- Coordinate with the design team, analyze website traffic.

If you're a customer support lead:

- Answer escalated support tickets
- Train new support agents
- Update the support FAQ

- Analyze ticket trends
- Coordinate with engineering on bug reports.

Everyone's task map will look different. The goal is capturing the essence of *what you do* day-to-day.

STEP 2

Next to each task, mark **H**, **M**, or **L** for High, Medium, or Low exposure to automation.

- **High (H)**: you suspect an AI or machine could do it now or very soon.
- **Medium (M)**: AI might do parts of it or could in the near future.
- **Low (L)**: heavily relies on human elements that AI can't do well.

STEP 3

Circle **high exposure** tasks. These are priorities for either **delegating to AI** or **upskilling beyond**. Don't let your value to the organization lie in tasks AI can take over.

Can you automate any of them *yourself* right now? For example, if a lot of your time is spent generating reports, learn a tool or script to automate parts of that. This can free you to focus on interpreting results (a Medium or Low exposure aspect).

If a high task is scheduling, try a scheduling assistant tool. The mindset here is proactive. Better *you* automate tasks than someone automating you. Be the person who introduces efficiency. Transition into a more future-proof role. Be the one implementing AI, not being replaced by it.

Also, if a task is high exposure and not particularly value-adding, should it occupy less of your time going forward? For instance, automating data entry could free up hour each week for more strategic work.

STEP 4

Look at the **low exposure** tasks involving strategy, creativity, interpersonal skills, or complex problem-solving.

Ask: how can I do *more* of these? Shift the balance of your role toward the things AI can't do. If "client communication" or "creative strategy" is on your list as low and you currently only spend 10% of your time on it, can you increase that? Maybe volunteer for a project that requires those human skills.

If you marked "mentoring junior staff" as low, because it's people-centric, but it's not formally part of your job, maybe you can start doing it informally–to build your leadership and management skills, which are needed in roles resilient roles.

Think about how to **enrich your role with more low-exposure tasks**. This makes you harder to replace and usually makes work more interesting and fulfilling. Because those tasks tend to be more meaningful.

STEP 5

Identify **new skills** or tasks you could add to your repertoire that align with resilient characteristics.

- Data storytelling: Learn how to take data that AI can crunch and weave it into a narrative for decision-makers–a human skill.
- Manual to tech blend: If you're in a hands-on role,

consider learning how to program or operate the robots and systems being introduced. Move from pure labor to a blend of labor and tech operation.

- Sales shift: If your role is mostly cold calls—high exposure—aim for account management that focuses on relationships—lower exposure.
- Warehouse shift: If your job is heavy physical labor—high exposure—train for roles like logistics coordinator or equipment maintenance specialist—lower exposure.

The idea is to *augment and pivot* your career, not do a random jump. Look at the direction your industry is heading and aim for in-demand roles. Picture your role in two years if you **shed some high-exposure tasks** by automating or delegating them. **Then doubled down on low-exposure tasks**. What would a day in that job look like? Does it look more valuable and interesting? That's a direction to pursue. Does it look empty—meaning if you automated everything you do, nothing would remain— that's a sign to transition to a different role with a healthier task mix.

One outcome of this exercise might be identifying adjacent roles that are inherently more resilient.

Suppose you're a graphic designer doing a lot of production artwork, which AI can partly automate. In mapping, you realize the parts you love are low exposure—conceptual discussions with clients and marketing strategy. That points to **brand strategist** or **art director** role. Jobs that use your design knowledge but feature high-level ideas and client interaction are hard for AI to replace.

Are you a junior accountant spending time on entries—high exposure—but who enjoys interpreting numbers?

Aim for **financial analyst** or **business analyst**, where explaining *why* the numbers are what they are is key and more human-driven.

The goal is **not** to do this exercise once and forget it. You can revisit every 6-12 months as technology, and your work keep evolving. Make it a habit. Recalibrate your task exposure and adjust course as needed. That way, you avoid complacency.

Don't be caught off guard when a part of your job gets automated. See it coming and be ready.

Do This Now: Future-Proof Your Role

Protect your career by acting on your role's exposure.

Audit Your Job Tasks Using the Exercise Above

Identify one *High-exposure* task you can start to automate or delegate to technology *this month*. Even if it's small—an Excel macro or an AI tool to reduce manual work. It will build your automation skill and free up time.

Enrich Your Role With A Low-Exposure Task

Volunteer for or propose one project that involves creativity, complex problem-solving, or human interaction.

If you work back-office, volunteer to join a cross-department team where you'll interact and collaborate (social skills arena). If you're technical, take on a task that requires creative design thinking or user experience input.

Add one people-or idea-focused responsibility to your plate.

Explore An Adjacent Resilient Role

Research a job one step higher on the "resilient" scale than yours.

If you're a customer support rep (high exposure), look at roles like customer success manager or community manager. These focus more on relationship-building and less on repetitive problem fixing. What skills or certifications do those require?

Make a simple plan for gaining one of those skills (online course, shadowing someone, etc.).

Explore An Adjacent Resilient Role

Research a job one step higher on the "resilient" scale than yours.

If you're a customer support rep (high exposure), look at roles like customer success manager or community manager. These focus more on relationship-building and less on repetitive problem fixing. What skills or certifications do those require?

Make a simple plan for gaining one of those skills (online course, shadowing someone, etc.).

Double Down on a Human-Centric Skills

Pick a soft/human skill—communication, negotiation, project leadership, empathy in management, etc.—that you want to strengthen.

Dedicate time to it. Read a book or take a short course on that skill. For example, effective communication is a timeless asset. Improving it will pay off in any job, especially those AI can't do.

Network With People In Resilient Roles

Identify someone in your circle (or a friend-of-a-friend) who works in a field considered resilient (nurse, product manager, creative director, etc.).

Have coffee or virtual chat. Ask them how they leverage uniquely human skills in their job and how tech is affecting them.

This can provide insight and confidence and expand your network into future-proof areas to open doors if you pivot.

By proactively mapping and steering your career, you transform fears of automation into strategies for innovation. Instead of bracing for impact, design your own professional evolution. Treating your career as a dynamic, steerable journey. This mindset could be the key resiliency trait in the AI age.

Bonus Extras

Ready to Go Deeper? Download Your Bonus Tools

You've just completed your career stocktake and explored what matters most in your work.

To make this process easier, I've created a set of companion tools you can use right now:

- **Career Stocktake Worksheet** - Capture your current role, skills in use, and skills you want to grow.
- **Strengths & Gaps Matrix** - Plot where your skills fit today's market demand and see what to double down on.
- **Role Alignment Checklist** - Quickly check how your role matches your values, goals, and lifestyle.
- **Vision Mapping Exercise** - Describe your ideal future role across skills, environment, and impact.
- **AI Prompt Companion** - Use pre-designed prompts to help uncover transferable skills, identify gaps, or explore new roles.

ACCESS THESE TOOLS AT:

https://go.habitkind.store/careeraccelerator

SCAN ME

These resources are designed to help you turn reflection into action right away.

Part II

THE 7 STEPS TO FUTURE-PROOF YOUR CAREER

Chapter 4
Step 1 Future-Proof Mindset

Alex's Monday started with a shock. After 20 years as an account manager, he watched a new AI system quietly take over tasks he'd done manually for years. At first, panic set in. Would the next algorithm take his job entirely? He imagined explaining to his family that his career had been erased by software.

Instead of spiraling, Alex pivoted, throwing himself into learning new digital tools. He even volunteered for a cross-functional AI project at work. What began as fear turned into determination. A year later, Alex is in a reinvented role guiding his team to leverage AI for client outreach.

He's not the most technical person in the company, but he is highly adaptable. His emotional resilience turned automation anxiety into opportunity. Alex demonstrates a simple but powerful mindset shift. Change isn't the end of your career. It can begin your evolution.

Why It Matters

Adaptability and resilience form the core of a future-proof mindset. In an age of rapid disruptions, they are essentially your personal job insurance. Machines excel at repetitive, predictable tasks but falter when things go off-script. When conditions change, algorithms fail or wait for human input.

You, however, can improvise. Adaptable people navigate new situations, learn on the fly, and devise creative solutions when old rules no longer apply. Emotional resilience makes such adaptability possible and keeps you steady during disruption. AI has no feelings to bruise, but also no grit. It can't "bounce back" after setbacks or get creative with a novel problem.

You can.

Resilience means absorbing shocks without breaking. It lets you turn a job loss into a chance to reinvent yourself, or a new tool into a chance to re-skill. Adaptability lets you work alongside automation rather than be run over by it.

It's the capacity to say, "Alright, the game changed—time to learn the new rules," instead of giving up. Resilience keeps your confidence intact through that learning curve. Together, these traits make you "automation-proof" because you keep evolving your role in ways robots cannot.

Evidence & Examples

The importance of adaptability isn't just feel-good rhetoric. It shows up in hard data and employer demands. The latest Future of Jobs survey found **"resilience, flexibility, and agility" among top five skills employers value** (WEF, 2023).

Companies predict that **44% of workers' core skills will change by 2027 due to technology advancements** (WEF, 2023). Nearly half of what you know could become obsolete in a few years. This is a clear signal that staying flexible and always learning is critical (WEF, 2023). Smart companies know adaptability beats fixed expertise in the long run.

Recent history demonstrates this. Consider the COVID-19 pandemic. In weeks, organizations had to reinvent processes and roles. Employees who adapted quickly became MVPs of their teams. They learned new digital collaboration tools, adjusted to remote workflows, took on new responsibilities. Those who said "that's not my job" or crumbled under stress were left behind.

Adaptability was the X-factor for job security during that crisis. And the same is proving true in today's AI-driven disruption. A McKinsey study's findings underscore this. **Under 5% of occupations can be fully automated. But one third of activities in 60% of jobs are automatable with current technology** (McKinsey, 2023).

Most jobs won't just vanish. They'll be *redefined* for those ready to seize new tasks. Roles will shift to higher-value work machines can't do.

Researchers estimate **3-14% of the global workforce, hundreds of millions of workers, needing to switch occupations or radically upgrade skills by 2030** due to automation's impact (Fennell, 2025).

Those who thrive won't see themselves as static job titles but as versatile bundles of skills to continually repurpose. We see this in disrupted industries.

Take retail: e-commerce and automation have eliminated many traditional sales roles. But adaptive workers transitioned into new roles like e-commerce specialist, customer experience manager, and supply chain analyst.

Their frontline knowledge was still valuable. It just had to be applied in new ways.

In manufacturing: as assembly lines introduced robotics, some workers resisted and feared change. Others volunteered to train with the new machines. Those who embraced new tech often kept their jobs.

They got promoted into roles like robot technicians or automation coordinators. They moved from repetitive tasks to supervising and optimizing the automated process, often at higher pay.

Roles don't just disappear. They *transform*. People who transform along with their roles prosper.

Emotional resilience underpins these success stories. Workers who panicked or dug in their heels found themselves obsolete. Workers who stayed calm, managed their stress, and approached change with curiosity became indispensable bridges between old and new.

No wonder employers report growing appreciation for workers who can handle stress and maintain positive attitudes amid change.

LinkedIn's workplace learning report consistently cites adaptability and resilience as among the top soft skills employers need for the future. One striking real-world case comes from **AT&T's massive reskilling initiative**.

Faced with many of its traditional telecom jobs becoming outdated, AT&T invested in retraining its workforce. Adaptable employees dove into the training. They shifted into new tech-centric domains like data science and cybersecurity. Those who refused to learn struggled or were let go.

With the right mindset and support, even mid-career professionals can pivot to new careers. They were willing to be beginners again, put in study hours, and overcome short-term challenges such as steep learning curves, pay cuts during retraining. But their resilience paid off with continued, future-ready careers.

Fast Learning Path: Building Adaptability & Resilience

You can cultivate adaptability and emotional resilience, like any other skill. Here's how to fast-track these abilities.

Embrace Micro-Changes

Deliberately switch up small routines to get comfortable with change. Try a new software tool, a different route to work, or a feature outside your typical duties. Low-stakes changes train your brain to handle the unfamiliar. Step outside your comfort zone to allow *change* to become routine.

Reframe Setbacks as Experiments

Failures and disruptions aren't the opposite of success. They're part of the path toward it. See them as experiments that produce data, not as catastrophes. Ask yourself, "What did I learn from this?"

Didn't get the promotion you wanted? Use it as a signal to grow, pick one new skill to build. Treat the experience as feedback, not a final judgment. Every setback becomes a stepping stone. This mindset builds resilience and keeps you moving forward.

Stress-Proof Your Routine

Develop a mental or physical wellness habit that helps you stay steady under stress. It could be a daily 10-minute meditation, a short jog, or a mid-afternoon walk.

Regular stress-release practices are pressure valves. When bigger changes hit, you'll have the emotional capacity to cope. Resilience isn't just mental. Your body and mind are linked. And healthy habits strengthen your overall ability to bounce back.

Stay Curious and Keep Learning

Make continuous learning your default response to change. When a new technology or process emerges in your field, commit to learning about it rather than avoiding it.

Adopt a beginner's mindset. Allow yourself to be curious instead of defensive. The habit of continuous learning not only expands your skills, boosting adaptability. It also proves to you that you can adapt and grow at any age, reinforcing confidence during future changes.

Do This Now: Adaptability & Resilience

Scan Your Horizon

Identify one emerging trend or technology in your industry that could impact your job in the near future. This week, find an article, webinar, or tutorial about it and engage with the content.

Even if it's outside your current role, getting **a preview of changes on the horizon** will prepare your mindset to adapt. Knowledge combats fear.

Do a Role Rotation (Mini-Version)

For one day, swap a task with a colleague from another team or department (with your manager's okay). If you're in marketing, shadowing a customer service rep or try out a basic data analysis task.

Stepping into a different role, even briefly, forces you to adapt to new workflows and perspectives. It flexes your adaptability muscle in a safe, supportive way.

Build a "Bounce-Back" Ritual

The next time you face a setback at work such as a failed project, tough feedback, practice a specific ritual to process it and move forward. Write in a journal for 10 minutes about what happened and what you'll do differently. Or debrief with a trusted mentor. **Having a go-to recovery method** prevents getting stuck in disappointment. Acknowledge the bump, learn from it, and refocus on the next step.

Fact Bombs: Adaptability & Resilience

Top Skill Demand

Adaptability-related traits (resilience, flexibility, agility) are among the **top five most valued skills** in today's workforce (WEF, 2023).

Skills Half-Life

Employers estimate **44% of workers' skills will need updating** by 2027, due to technology changes (WEF, 2023)—highlighting the need for constant learning.

Automation Impact

While under **5% of jobs are fully automatable**, in about **60% of jobs, 30% of tasks are automatable** with current tech (McKinsey, 2023). Most roles will evolve, not vanish. And adaptable workers will fill the newly shaped jobs.

Chapter 5
Step 2
Upgrade Constantly

Danielle's comfortable routine began to feel like a trap. A 38-year-old financial analyst, she realized one day that her five-year-old skills were suddenly in low demand. **New data analytics tools and AI-driven software were now standard in finance**. Her company was starting to favor candidates with fresh certifications.

At first, Danielle felt overwhelmed and even a bit resentful— had all her experience become obsolete overnight?

After being passed over for a high-profile project, she decided she would never feel stagnant again.

That same evening, Danielle enrolled in an online course on data science basics. Over the next six months, she spent nights and weekends hitting the books. She earned a well-regarded certification in financial analytics.

It wasn't easy balancing work, family, and learning, but the payoff was clear.

The next time a big project came up, Danielle's new skills made her the obvious choice to lead it. She became the go-to person in her team for training others on the latest tools. Fear that her knowledge was falling behind transformed into confidence that she could learn anything to stay ahead.

Danielle's story illustrates a powerful truth. In times of rapid change, **continuous upgrading is the only sustainable career strategy***.*

Why It Matters

"Upgrade Constantly" means adopting a lifelong learning mindset—continuously acquiring new knowledge, skills, and credentials to stay relevant. In the past, you might go to school, learn a profession, and then ride that skill set for decades. Today, that approach is career suicide.

The shelf-life of technical skills is shrinking fast, and entirely new skill sets emerge every few years (IBM, 2021). Waiting for knowledge to expire before you learn something new is like waiting for your phone's battery to die before charging it. Modern careers demand *proactive* learning. You charge yourself continuously.

This matters because automation and AI are constantly absorbing the lower-skill, routine job components. What's left are higher-value tasks—only available if you've **upgraded** your capabilities to handle them. Lifelong learning is an antidote to job insecurity. If you're always adding to your skill portfolio, you're less vulnerable to layoffs or industry downturns.

You become a **"versatilist" with broad, adaptive skill sets** that fit many roles. Continual learning keeps your mind adaptable and curious. It trains you to handle new challenges with confidence because you've built a habit of growth.

Committing to upgrade constantly is how you **future-proof *yourself***. It turns anxiety about change into action against obsolescence. It ensures you remain a sought-after professional, not a cautionary tale of stagnation.

Evidence & Examples

Data on the need for lifelong learning is striking. Reportedly, **six in ten workers will require additional training or reskilling by 2027. This is just to keep up with how technology is changing jobs**. Only about half of workers have access to adequate training opportunities (WEF, 2023).

This training gap shows both the demand and the challenge. There's a massive need for upskilling. Individuals often have to take the initiative.

Another telling statistic is that employers estimate **44% of workers' skills will be disrupted by 2027** (WEF, 2023). No wonder more employers are seeking workers with traits like *curiosity and lifelong learning* (WEF, 2023). Companies want people eager and able to learn continuously.

Also, formal credentials are no longer a one-and-done deal. The rise of online courses, professional certificates, and micro-degrees is a direct response to market hunger for continuous education. Platforms like Coursera, edX, and LinkedIn Learning report millions of mid-career learners enrolling every year. They earn new certifications in data analytics, project management, AI, and more.

Many employers now partner with such platforms or offer tuition reimbursement, recognizing that if their workforce doesn't keep learning, the company won't keep winning. IBM (2021) found that over **120 million workers in the world's 12 largest economies may need retraining in the next few years due to AI**. They also found a **5-year "half-life" for many professional skills**.

This is why IBM, Google, and other forward-looking

companies launch continuous learning programs (IBM's Digital Badge program, Google's internal "30% time" for learning). They encourage employees to constantly update skill toolkits.

Look how rapidly skill requirements have changed in just the past decade. Marketing roles now demand proficiency in data analytics and AI-driven ad platforms—skills most marketing majors didn't study 10 years ago.

Those who taught themselves or took extra courses on Google Analytics or AI-based marketing tools zoomed ahead in their careers. Those who said "that's not my area" found their prospects shrinking.

In manufacturing, technicians who learned how to program and maintain the new robotics and CNC machines became exponentially more valuable than those who stuck to the old manual processes.

In fields like healthcare, continuous upgrading is crucial. Nurses and doctors constantly train on new devices and treatment methods to ensure patient care and to meet licensing requirements.

The **Bureau of Labor Statistics** found that today's workforce holds more jobs over a lifetime than for previous generations. It undergoes more skill requirement transitions within each job.

On average, U.S. workers in their 30s have already changed jobs multiple times and often pivoted their skill focus at least once. Journalists learn multimedia and coding, and salespeople become adept in CRM software and data analysis.

Continuous learning isn't just about chasing the newest tech skill. It's also about deepening your expertise and broadening your perspective. AT&T created the Workforce 2020 initiative, investing $1 billion in employee education. They offered training in new skills like data science, cybersecurity, and cloud computing.

Employees took online courses, earned nanodegrees (small, specialized online certifications), and transitioned into entirely new roles within the company. They filled many high-skill jobs instead of being laid off. They "future-proofed" their careers by leveling up instead of languishing.

Another example: Jorge a mid-career mechanical engineer found his role increasingly overlapping with software. Instead of resisting, he took night classes in programming.

Within two years, he evolved into a hybrid mech/software engineer, leading IoT (Internet of Things) projects at his firm. He credits his promotion and job security to that extra learning. Younger graduates entering the field had both sets of skills by default. He knew he had to catch up or risk falling behind.

These stories underline a common theme. **Careers are no longer ladders**. They're climbing walls. You don't just go up. Sometimes you go sideways to grab a new skill that will ultimately lift you higher.

The constant in all this is learning. It's the nutrient for a growing career. As one CEO put it, "The most important skill is the skill of learning new skills." Evidence is everywhere that lifelong learning isn't optional. It's the price of admission to tomorrow's opportunities.

Fast Learning Path: Embracing Lifelong Learning

Lifelong learning might sound abstract. But you can build it into your life with concrete habits. Here's how to upgrade yourself continually.

Schedule Learning Time

Treat learning like an important meeting with yourself. Dedicate small, regular time slots (30 minutes a day or a few hours a week) to learning a new skill or concept.

Consistency beats cramming. Schedule "Learning Hour" every Tuesday and Thursday after work to take an online course or read industry journals. Over a year, those hours add up to lots of new knowledge.

Micro-Learn Every Day

Include bite-sized learning in your daily routine. Listen to podcasts while commuting. Watch a 10-minute how-to video during lunch. Do a quick interactive lesson on a learning app before bed.

Done daily, this will compound. Many apps and websites offer "daily learning snacks" in coding, language learning, business, etc. Subscribe to one relevant to your field. Keep your brain in continuous upgrade mode.

Pursue Stretch Assignments

Volunteer for projects at work outside your current expertise. This pressure can force you to learn by doing. Is your company implementing new software, entering a new market?

Raise your hand to be involved. You might have to scramble to pick up some skills on the fly, but that's exactly the point. It's on-the-job upskilling.

Leverage Free Resources

Today, lots of learning is low-cost or free. Take advantage of MOOCs (Massive Open Online Courses) from platforms like Coursera or edX to audit courses for free.

Use YouTube's wealth of tutorials or free coding academies and libraries. Cost should not be a barrier. List three reputable free learning resources in your profession. Try them over the next few months to see which fits your style.

Keep a "To-Learn" List

Maintain a running list of things you want to learn or know more about—be it a software, methodology, or a soft skill. Whenever you encounter a gap ("I wish I knew about X"), add it to the list. Systematically tackle those items one by one. This turns nebulous thoughts into an actionable agenda. And crossing things off your learning list gives a sense of progress.

Do This Now: Lifelong Learning & Upskilling

Enroll in One Course

Find short online courses or workshops on skills that would benefit your career or that intrigue you and enroll *this week*. Try certification in emerging tools, webinars on leadership, or data literacy classes. Commit money or time investments in yourself.

By registering, you turn a vague intention into a concrete plan.

Set a Reading Goal

Identify one highly regarded book in your field or field you aspire to enter and set a goal to read it in the next month.

Break it down by chapters per week. If you're in marketing, try a book on AI in marketing; if you're in finance, maybe one on fintech innovations.

Reading expert overviews will enhance your understanding, sparking ideas for further skills to learn.

Join a Professional Community

This week, join a professional network or forum (online or offline) related to a skill you want to develop—a LinkedIn group, Slack community, or local meetup. Introduce yourself and engage in one discussion.

Interacting with people learning the same thing creates accountability and exposes you to new learning resources. For instance, if you want to learn coding, join a GitHub project or a beginner's coding forum. Contribute or ask a question.

Apply a New Skill Immediately

Take something you've recently learned and use it in your current job *within the next two weeks*. Use a new Excel function. Try a communication technique from a management article. Write a small script to automate a task.

Don't wait for full mastery—applying new knowledge in real life cements learning and proves its value. If it's not directly applicable at work, incorporate it into a personal project.

The key is to move from learning to doing, reinforcing the upgrade.

Fact Bombs: Lifelong Learning

Reskilling Revolution

Over **60% of workers** will need retraining or upskilling by 2027 to meet changing job demands (WEF, 2023). Employers are urgently seeking self-driven learners as the half-life of job skills shortens dramatically.

Skill Disruption Ahead

Executives estimate **44% of employee skills will be disrupted** by 2028 (WEF, 2023). Staying relevant means **continuously updating your toolkit**.

ROI of Learning

Studies show that companies embracing continuous learning see greater innovation and productivity. IBM (2021) found that organizations with strong training programs are **more productive and can close skills gaps faster**.

It predicted **120 million workers** in major economies may need to be retrained in the next few years due to AI. This spotlights how widespread and critical lifelong learning has become.

Chapter 6
Step 3
AI + You

Elena hit a wall in her job search. Months of sending out resumes yielded only generic rejection emails. Frustrated, she tried a different approach–a free AI resumes assistant to analyze job descriptions and tailor her resumes for each role with the right keywords.

She practiced common interview questions with an AI chatbot, refining her answers and reducing her anxiety. Within weeks, the response to her applications shifted. She landed multiple interview calls. One recruiter praised the clarity of her resume.

Ultimately, Elena secured a role at a company she'd thought out of reach. When she asked the hiring manager what made her stand out, the manager mentioned her well-crafted resume and confident interview. Elena quietly smiled, knowing she had a secret collaborator in her success.

Her story shows how embracing AI as a personal career tool can turn a stalled job hunt into a fast track to the next level.

Why It Matters

We've entered an era where working smarter means working with AI, not against it. 'AI + You' is about using AI as a tool to augment your skills and boost your career, from finding job opportunities faster to enhancing your day-to-day performance.

Why does this matter? Because employers are increasingly bringing AI to their side of the table. Recruiters use AI to scan resumes, and algorithms rank candidates. Hiring managers use AI tools to evaluate interview responses.

If you're not AI savvy, you're flying blind in a game where the other side has high-tech vision.

On the flip side, **AI can supercharge your job search and career development**. It can be your personal research assistant, resume editor, interview coach, and personal skills trainer.

In practical terms, that means more easily uncovering job openings matching your profile. It means optimizing your application materials to get past automated filters. It means preparing you for interviews with data-driven insights.

Evidence & Examples

AI use on the hiring end is skyrocketing, with **companies increasingly including AI in HR and recruitment** (SHRM, 2025). Many large firms use AI-powered Applicant Tracking Systems (ATS) to filter resumes before humans ever see them. These systems look for key terms related to skills and experience.

If you aren't aware of this, you might never hear back because your resume wasn't tuned to AI criteria. Savvy candidates optimize their resumes and LinkedIn profiles with the right keywords so that algorithms elevate them.

Reportedly, **87% of recruiters use LinkedIn to source and vet candidates** (Next Gen Personal Finance [NGPF], 2023). LinkedIn uses AI to suggest candidates to recruiters. Ensuring your profile is complete with relevant skills listed, greatly increases your chances of getting noticed (NGPF, 2023).

AI is becoming a job-seeker's best friend. Some 46% of 1000 surveyed job seekers used **AI to write or improve their resumes and cover letters**. Some **78%** of those **got an interview** (Resume Builder [RB], 2023). This isn't just a fluke— AI can help tailor your applications to each job, making them more compelling.

If you paste a job description into an AI tool, it can highlight skills to emphasize on your resume, like a career coach. Reportedly, *69% of AI-assisted candidates saw overall higher response rates from employers* (RB, 2023). Using AI tools in your application process can significantly improve outcomes, as Elena's story illustrates.

Over **70% of recently surveyed leaders prefer candidates with strong AI skills and less experience to more experienced candidates with no AI skills** (Microsoft, 2024). That's a remarkable shift. AI skills can outweigh years of experience.

Similarly, 66% of those leaders would only hire people with some AI know-how (Microsoft, 2024). These stats underscore that AI literacy (even at a user level) is seen as a core professional skill.

Real-world examples bring these numbers to life. A recent MBA graduate used an AI tool to analyze the public financial reports of a company before her interview. It helped her ask impressively pointed questions. She got the job and the interviewer later commented on her exceptional preparation.

The pattern is clear. **Those who adopt AI tools early tend to leap ahead**. They have more time for creative and strategic work because AI takes care of grunt tasks. They make data-driven decisions in seconds, where others might take hours. They impress bosses and clients with responsiveness and insight.

Those who ignore these tools risk falling behind, doing work at yesterday's pace and precision. **"AI + You"** is not a futuristic concept—it's here and now. Embracing it can be the career turbocharger that sets you apart in both hiring and performance.

Fast Learning Path: Becoming an AI-Augmented Professional

You don't need to be a programmer or data scientist to start using AI for your career. You just need to practice integrating AI into your routine. Here's how to quickly get up to speed.

Explore AI Job Tools

Identify and try out one AI tool relevant to your job hunt or career. Use an AI resume reviewer to analyze your resume for improvements. Try LinkedIn features like AI-written profile suggestions or the interview preparation tool. Hands-on use will demystify AI. For the next position you apply to use at least one AI feature to optimize your application.

Practice Prompting

If you're using a chatbot AI like ChatGPT, practice drafting clear and specific prompts to get better results. Think of it as giving instructions to a very smart intern.

Don't just say, "Help me with my resume." Detail what you need. "Here is my resume and a job description. How can I tweak my resume to better match this job posting?"

The more precisely you prompt, the more useful the response. *Prompt craft* is a skill you can develop. Try writing the same query a few different ways to test which produce the best outputs.

Stay Updated on AI Features

AI capabilities are evolving rapidly. Stay informed about new AI features in tools you already use. If you use Microsoft or Google products, pay attention to announcements about Microsoft Copilot or Gemini features in Google Workspace. Subscribe to a tech newsletter or follow a LinkedIn group about AI in your industry. Awareness ensures you won't miss out when a game-changing tools and features arrives.

Simulate Before You're in the Hot Seat

Leverage AI to simulate high-pressure scenarios in advance. If you have a presentation coming up, use an AI speech coach to get feedback on clarity and pacing. If you're heading into an interview, have a chatbot pretend to be the interviewer and ask you tough questions. This low-stakes practice can improve real performance and build skill and confidence.

Do This Now: Leverage AI for Career Growth

Audit Your Online Presence with AI

Copy-paste your LinkedIn profile (or resume) into a generative AI tool and ask, "What roles or keywords is this profile suited for? What could be improved to appeal to recruiters in [your industry]?" Implement one concrete update from the feedback, like adding a specific skill or rewording your headline. This can help align your personal brand with what algorithms (and recruiters) look for.

Use AI for Interview Prep

Take three common interview questions for your desired role (for example, "Tell me about yourself," "Describe a challenging project," "How do you handle deadlines?"). Feed them into an AI like ChatGPT along with your answers and the prompt "Critique this interview answer and suggest improvements."

You'll get suggestions on making your responses stronger. Practice incorporating the feedback and saying your refined answers out loud. By doing this, you benefit from instant coaching to polish your interview performance.

Set an AI Learning Goal

Commit to learning the basics of one AI platform relevant to your field.

If you're in marketing, familiar yourself with an AI content generator tool. If you're in finance, explore an AI forecasting or analysis tool.

Sign up for a free trial or find a tutorial and spend at least two hours this week learning its functions.

By the end of the week, create a small project for yourself using the tool. Marketers can generate a sample social media post calendar. Analysts can have AI process a sample dataset.

This concrete goal moves you from "I should learn AI" to getting your hands dirty, learning what could become your secret weapon at work.

Fact Bombs: AI + Career

AI in Hiring

Some **35%-45% of recently surveyed companies** have adopted AI in hiring. In multiple surveys, 85% or more employers say it saves them time and boosts efficiency (SHRM, 2025). If you use AI in your own job search, you're keeping pace with how jobs are being filled.

Job Seekers Using AI

Nearly **half of job seekers (46%)** in a recent survey use AI tools like ChatGPT to help write resumes and cover letters. Among them, **78% got interviews** with AI-assisted applications (RB, 2023). Using AI in your application can significantly improve your chances of landing an interview.

AI Skills = Career Currency

Seventy-one percent of surveyed business leaders would hire less-experienced candidates with strong AI skills over more experienced candidates without them (Microsoft, 2024). **66% would not** hire someone with no AI skills at all.

Demonstrating even basic AI proficiency on your resume or in interviews can give you a serious competitive edge in today's job market.

Chapter 7
Step 4 Work Smarter with AI

Now that you've turbocharged your career development with AI, it's time to bring that advantage into your daily work life. In this chapter, we move from landing the job to thriving in it—using AI as your partner in everyday productivity and collaboration.

Nathan manages a customer support team. He used to spend hours every week manually sorting and assigning support tickets. It was tedious work that pulled him away from bigger-picture improvements.

Frustrated by constant backlog, Nathan tried something new. He tried an AI-driven ticket assistant to read incoming requests and suggest priorities and category tags. At first, some team members were skeptical.

But Nathan learned how to "coach" the AI with better prompts and rules. Soon, the tool was accurately handling routine tickets and flagging only the complex issues for humans. Nathan's team saw their response time double.

With freed-up hours, he coached his staff on handling tough cases and improved the help website to cut down on basic queries. Customer satisfaction rose and Nathan's role transformed.

He went from overworked supervisor to strategic problem-solver. He got recognition from upper management for a jump in team productivity. Through daily AI collaboration, Nathan unlocked new levels of efficiency. His story shows how human oversight plus AI power is a winning combo.

Why It Matters

"Work Smarter with AI" is about using AI to amplify day-to-day productivity and creativity. The goal is not to work harder or longer. It's to leverage AI so you can focus on the most human, high-value parts of your job.

This matters because **productivity is the currency of success in every workplace**. And AI can dramatically boost it.

AI can automate or accelerate repetitive or data-heavy tasks that eat up time, from drafting reports, to sorting data, scheduling meetings, or answering common emails. Offloading drudgery to machines frees up time for creative, strategic, and interpersonal aspects of work that **only you can do**.

It's like having a tireless personal assistant or a junior team member who works 24/7. AI can serve as a collaborator that brings in fresh ideas or solutions. An AI tool might suggest code or design mockups or marketing copy variations. And you select or refine the best ones.

Human-AI collaboration means you're no longer limited to what you can personally brainstorm or execute. You have a force multiplier.

Learn to work smart with AI to accomplish more in less time and reduce errors. AI can catch mistakes or inconsistencies and help you adapt faster to new challenges.

In a team setting, everybody using AI to handle routine stuff can increase team capacity, overall performance, and innovation.

On the flip side, if you don't tap into these tools, you risk falling behind your colleagues or competitors who produce twice the output or respond twice as fast.

In the AI age, working smarter is the antidote to feeling overwhelmed. It's how you surf the wave of information and tasks rather than drown in it.

Evidence & Examples

Productivity gains from AI assistance are not just anecdotal. They're being measured and they're huge. Across multiple studies in different fields, AI tools have been shown to boost worker throughput significantly—by an average of 66% (Nielsen, 2023). For example:

- Customer support agents using an AI assistant handled nearly **14% more inquiries per hour**—the equivalent of gaining an extra hour+ of work in an eight-hour day without working longer.
- Business professionals tasked with writing (such as press releases and emails) produced **59% more content per hour** with AI assistance.
- In a programming trial, developers using AI completed **2× more coding tasks** compared to those without AI.

These aren't small improvements. They're transformative. They show that by integrating AI into your workflow, you can potentially double your productivity. Or you can output what previously took a whole team to do.

Quality remains critical and AI can help there too. For routine tasks, AI reduces human error by handling the rote stuff consistently. Even for complex work, studies found that outputs created with AI assistance can be higher quality. In one study, writing with AI assistance was rated higher on a 7-point quality scale (Nielsen, 2023).

AI can provide a solid first draft or raw material, which humans can refine—with the final product more polished than either could accomplish alone (Nielsen, 2023). AI handles the first 80%, and you add the crucial 20% of finesse and critical thought.

Employers recognize this synergy. Many companies now explicitly encourage workers to use AI tools to enhance output, much like they encouraged using computers and the internet in earlier decades.

In a survey by Microsoft (2024), **78% of workers reported "bringing their own AI" (BYOAI).** People are relying on AI to help them cope with heavy workloads—68% of participants struggled with work volume and looked to AI for relief. Clearly, there's a grassroots movement to work smarter with AI, even before top-down policies catch up.

Companies that have embraced it are seeing results. One report noted that **92% of participating companies piloting AI in HR already see benefits** (BCG, 2024). **And over 10% reported more than 30% productivity gains**. Where AI is applied thoughtfully, significant efficiency gains often follow. Consider some concrete examples across different jobs type.

- **Project Managers**: AI tools can automatically update schedules when tasks change and even predict when projects are at risk for delay. With these insights, managers can act earlier than if relying on manual tracking.

- **Financial Analysts**: AI reconciles accounts and flags anomalies at lightning speed compared to manual checks, helping teams close the books in days instead of weeks.
- **Graphic Designers**: AI generates draft visuals or suggests layouts—work that once required a team of assistants—dramatically shortening concept development time.
- **Journalists**: AI pulls data or summarizes background info instantly, allowing reporters to focus more on storytelling and analysis.

Collaboration is being supercharged by AI. Language models are bringing down language barriers among global teams with real-time translation and even tone adjustment tools to help colleagues communicate more clearly.

AI can transcribe and summarize meetings, draft meeting minutes, highlight action items, and send follow-up reminders. Imagine finishing a meeting and within minutes every participant receives a summary of decisions and their tasks. That's happening now with AI meeting assistants. Teams can spend less time on administrivia and more on creative problem-solving.

For example, Rahul, a project manager, integrated an AI scheduling assistant into his routine to sort through team availability and automatically draft meeting agendas. His team noticed he was on top of every detail and didn't waste time in meetings. His "secret" was that AI helper running in the background. He was able to handle a larger team and more projects than other project managers, contributing to him getting promoted to senior project manager.

However, working smarter with AI isn't magic—it's a skill. Those who get the most out of AI learn *to prompt and guide* these tools effectively. AI is a "force multiplier."

> **Vague Instructions = Basic Help**
> **Clear, Detailed Instructions = Stellar Support**

Learning how to communicate with AI with good examples or step-by-step prompts, is the new workplace literacy. Companies are even training staff on "prompt engineering" so employees can harness AI better. Early adopters know that an AI coworker needs coaching. Humans who invest time to learn this are leaping ahead in productivity.

Evidence is everywhere that AI, when used wisely, can dramatically increase productivity and effectiveness at work. It can cut drudgery, improve quality, and multiply the impact of your effort. Those who integrate AI into daily work achieve more and position themselves as indispensable in an AI-augmented future.

Fast Learning Path: Supercharging Your Productivity with AI

You can start working smarter with AI by making it a natural part of how you tackle tasks. Here's how to build that capability quickly.

Begin with a Daily AI Habit

Pick one daily task and use an AI tool to assist with it every day for a week. Consider drafting your team's daily update email with an AI writing assistant. Or use an AI scheduling tool for your meetings.

By the end of the week, AI will be part of your routine. You'll see what it's good at—and where it falls short. Then ask yourself: did it save you time or mental energy? If yes, expand it to more tasks.

Learn to Craft Effective Prompts

Spend time experimenting with asking AI for help. Try the following prompt formula: give context, be specific about the task, and define the format of the answer.

For example, instead of saying, "Summarize this report," say "Summarize the key findings of this report in five bullet points, focusing on how they impact our marketing strategy."

Notice how the output changes. By practicing and comparing, you'll develop intuition for phrasing prompts that get the most useful responses.

Use AI as a Second Pair of Eyes

Make it a habit to run important work through an AI check. Finished a presentation deck? Ask AI critique it or suggest improvements. Wrote a chunk of code? Have AI review it for errors or edge cases. Drafted an email to a client? Let AI suggest a more concise version.

Treat AI like a colleague who proofreads and gives feedback. This will catch mistakes and teach you new ways to improve your work.

Automate Simple Workflows

Identify one multi-step process you do that could be partially automated with AI or basic scripts. If you always copy data from emails into a spreadsheet, use an AI email parser or a macro to do it.

If you generate weekly reports, see if your software has an AI feature to generate a first draft. Even simple built-in automations count. For example, Outlook and Gmail can suggest email replies, or Excel and Google Sheets can generate formulas or summaries with AI. These "small wins" free up time without needing extra tech tools.

Pro Tip: If you're unsure how to phrase a formula or set up a feature, ask AI directly. Just type something like "Write a formula in Excel that adds this column" or "Draft a polite reply to this email." The AI does the technical part for you.

Start small. The goal is to get comfortable linking tools to eliminate manual steps. Once you feel the time saved, you'll be motivated to automate more.

Collaborate with AI in Brainstorming

Next time you have to develop ideas—for a project name, a marketing tagline, or solutions to a problem—include an AI tool in your brainstorming. Prompt it for 5 or 10 suggestions.

You might discard many, but you could find a new spark or angle. This isn't about AI replacing your creativity; it's about boosting your idea generation.

Over time, you'll see AI as a creative partner for overcoming blank-page syndrome or exploring outside-the-box options quickly.

Do This Now: Daily AI Productivity Boost

Write 3 Better Prompts

Pick a task you could use help with tomorrow—summarizing a document, drafting a response, or analyzing data. Write a basic prompt to an AI for that task.

Now, instead of guessing on your own, ask the AI: "How could I improve this prompt to get a clearer or more useful response?" Try the AI's suggestions. Rewrite your prompt in at least two refined ways—add details, specify style, or focus on outcomes.

Finally, test each version. Compare the outputs and notice which gives the best results. This exercise can train you to communicate effectively with AI, so you get quality assistance, when you need it.

Set Up an AI Meeting Helper

If you have any team meetings or recurring meetings this week, use an AI tool to help with one aspect. Use an AI transcription service (many video conference apps have one built-in) to record and transcribe the meeting.

Or volunteer to use AI to draft the meeting agenda or summary. Doing this now will save you and your colleagues time. No more scrambling to take notes or wondering who said what. And it introduces AI into your team's workflow in helpful, low-risk ways.

Create an Email/Chat Template with AI

Identify a type of email or chat message you send frequently (status update, request for information, scheduling, etc.). Use AI to draft a general template for it.

For example, tell the AI, "Draft a polite email to request an update from a colleague on a project, in 3 sentences." Edit the AI's output to fit your tone and needs and save this as a template.

Next time you need to send a similar message, you'll only tweak a few details. Do this for one type of message today, and you'll shave minutes off future occurrences—small savings that add up.

Try an AI Planning Buddy

At the start of your next workday, spend five minutes with an AI assistant to plan your day. List your top tasks and ask the AI, "Help me prioritize these tasks: [list tasks with any deadlines or estimated effort]." It might suggest an order or even time blocks.

You can also ask, "What's a more efficient way to handle [task]?" for one item on your list. Even if you don't follow the AI's plan exactly, structuring your day with AI input can introduce new productivity hacks that you can implement immediately.

Fact Bombs: AI Productivity

Dramatic Productivity Leap

In field trials, workers using AI tools accomplished work significantly faster. Customer support agents handled **14% more queries/hour**. Writers produced **59% more content/hour**. And programmers completed **2X the coding tasks** in the same time (Nielsen, 2023). AI isn't just a minor efficiency tweak. It can potentially *double* output in complex tasks.

Quality and Speed

AI-assisted work isn't just faster, it can be *better* (Nielsen, 2023). AI can catch errors or suggest improvements, raising the bar on work quality while also speeding it up.

"BYOAI" Trend

Workers are so eager to lighten their load that **78% are bringing their own AI to work, sometimes without waiting for permission** (Microsoft, 2024). This is a sign that using AI to work smarter is becoming an employee-driven revolution. Those who jump on this trend responsibly can outperform peers and make themselves indispensable.

Chapter 8
Step 5
Double Down on Human Skills

    Maya's freelance career nearly ended when one of her biggest clients replaced her with an AI text generator for their blog content. At first, she was stunned and anxious. How could she compete with a machine that writes a dozen articles in a minute?

Maya even tried to match AI volume and speed, pushing herself to churn out content until she burned out. Then she realized she was fighting on the wrong battlefield. Instead of trying to beat the AI at its strength, she doubled down on her **human strengths**.

Maya began offering her clients something AI couldn't: strategic story-driven content infused with empathy. She hopped on calls with clients to deeply understand their brand voice and their audience's feelings. She even used AI for rough drafts, but then wove in humor, personal anecdotes, and emotional resonance that only a human could provide.

The result was that her content started performing better than purely AI-generated output. One client returned, saying "The AI writes articles, but you communicate meaning and connect with our readers."

Maya won back business and gained new clients who tried all-AI content and found it fell flat. By leaning into her uniquely human skills–understanding people and creative storytelling–Maya made herself more valuable than ever in the age of automation.

Why It Matters

In a world where AI is handling more tasks, your human skills become your superpowers. Machines can't easily replicate qualities like:

- **Creativity**–driving innovation and fresh ideas

- **Empathy**–building trust and connection
- **Critical Thinking**–sharpening assumptions and sound decisions
- **Ethical Judgment**–guiding choices where values matter
- **Communication**–shaping ideas so others act on them

As automation expands, these skills become the differentiators—ensuring you and AI are stronger together.

The work left over is often complicated. Human creativity, problem-solving, and emotional intelligence will always be in demand. AI can generate dozens of marketing slogans, but only a human can pick one that customers relate to and adjust it with cultural sensitivity or humor.

Chatbots might answer basic customer questions. But human customer service reps are needed when a situation is nuanced, or a customer is upset and needs empathy. AI can crunch numbers and detect patterns. But **critical thinking** is needed to ask the right questions, challenge assumptions, and make ethical decisions. AI won't question if data is biased or a recommendation is morally sound. Humans should.

Doubling down on human skills is how you differentiate yourself in the workforce, how you ensure that you and AI are stronger together. These human skills are transferable. Apply them across roles and industries. Maximize your career adaptability. Many surveys found that **increasingly employers value soft skills** as much as technical ones in hiring and promotions (McKinsey, 2024).

Being technically proficient isn't enough. To lead or to advance, you need the "human factor." Machines can't easily replicate:

- **Creativity**–fueling innovation
- **Empathy**–strengthening teamwork and customer relationships
- **Critical Thinking**–guiding complex decisions

Hone these skills where humans have an edge. They're your best path to future-proofing your role.

AI may be tireless and data-driven, but it has no imagination, no compassion, no wisdom. Those are *your* domain. In this step, amplify what makes you human and valuable.

Evidence & Examples

The case for human skills is backed by strong evidence from the job market and research. In the **Future of Jobs** report, human-centric skills stay top of the list. In 2023, "analytical thinking" and "creative thinking" were the top two most important skills to employers, followed by self-management skills like resilience, flexibility, and agility (WEF, 2023).

Empathy and active listening featured in the top 10 skills for the future. They are growing fast in importance because machines struggle with them. As such, the need for **curiosity, lifelong learning/adaptability,** and **resilience** saw big jumps in employer surveys (WEF, 2023).

Researchers estimate that by 2030, demand for social and emotional skills will rise by 26% in the U.S. (22% in Europe) across all industries (McKinsey, 2018). Demand for higher-level cognitive skills (creativity, complex problem-solving, critical thinking) is projected to grow by 19% in the U.S. by 2030 (McKinsey, 2018).

These forecasts suggest that as automation takes over basic tasks, the relative need for human judgment, creativity, and social interaction will grow significantly. Skills like *empathy, leadership, and initiative* are among the fastest growing because "machines are a long way from mastering" them (McKinsey, 2018).

We see this on the ground as well. When chatbots and AI customer service agents became common, some thought human customer service jobs would disappear. Instead, many companies refocused their human agents on the complex or high-stakes interactions requiring emotional intelligence.

Customer satisfaction often hinges on those human touches. PwC found that **82% of U.S. consumers want more human interaction in customer service**, especially when they have a problem and get frustrated with only interacting with technology. That's a big clue that empathy and communication are not just niceties. They affect the bottom line.

In health care, AI does diagnostic analysis, scanning images or patient data faster than any human. But patients consistently rate their care experience higher when they feel their doctor listens and shows concern.

Healthcare organizations are doubling down on empathy **training for practitioners**, aware that tech can't replace bedside manner. In studies, doctors who scored high on empathy had significantly better patient outcomes and lower rates of malpractice claims. Empathy can have real life-or-death impacts that AI can't replicate.

Critical thinking and the ability to judge information is another big one. AI can output authoritative-sounding reports. But they might be completely wrong or biased. Without human critical thinking, errors can propagate. Take the case of a financial AI used to predict loan approvals. It worked well until it started denying loans to qualified candidates because of hidden biases in data.

It took human analysts to spot the pattern, question it, and adjust the criteria. Employers know they need human oversight to interpret and challenge AI outputs. That's why executives often list critical thinking and problem-solving in the top skills they seek.

LinkedIn's 2024 Workplace Learning Report found companies focused on **combining technical skills with stronger soft skills**. Critical thinking and communication, which drive effective technology use, were especially in demand.

Let's not forget *creativity*. We've seen AI produce art, music, and writing. Yet, human creativity remains special. It often comes from personal experience, emotions, and cross-pollination of ideas.

That is, AI doesn't truly "understand." AI can remix the past. But humans create genuinely novel leaps, often by breaking rules or with intuitive flashes, not in datasets. Organizations crave innovation. And innovation springs from creative human minds.

A Deloitte report noted that as routine tasks are automated, relative time spent on creative work by employees is rising. And **companies that foster creativity outperform those that don't**. They cite examples like the auto manufacturer that automated assembly line tasks and then retrained workers to focus on quality improvements and efficiency. The company leveraged their firsthand knowledge. They turned factory workers into innovators on the floor.

Real world story. Consider the field of law. AI can now search case law and draft legal documents—tasks once done by junior lawyers. But top attorneys aren't prized for memorizing precedents; they're valued for strategic thinking, persuasive argumentation, and sound judgment.

Picture a junior lawyer who uses AI to handle the research but then applies critical thinking to craft winning strategies. That lawyer is far more valuable than one who can cite a hundred cases but lacks courtroom presence or judgment.

That's why law schools emphasize moot courts—practicing argument, persuasion, and judgment. Firms also mentor young attorneys on real-world judgment calls. These are the human elements that AI can't replace.

Another story. Jake, a UX (user experience) designer, discovered that AI could churn out interface mockups in seconds. But while they looked polished, they often felt generic. What set Jake apart was his human-centered approach. He interviewed users, listened to their frustrations, and translated that insight into designs that felt intuitive and delightful.

AI might generate a starting point, but it couldn't replace Jake's empathy or creativity. His ability to connect with people and shape experiences around their needs became the difference-maker. Clients noticed that his work, even when simpler, earned stronger feedback than cookie-cutter

AI designs. They valued not just a product, but the human touch only Jake could bring.

This is the **"secret sauce" of human insight** *and employers are taking notice.*

The common thread in these stories is simple: human skills amplify the impact of technical tools. As routine work gets automated, the uniquely human qualities—creativity, empathy, judgment—become the competitive edge.

Employers know it. Many hiring managers now use behavioral interviews or assessments specifically to gauge soft skills. And many are finding a "soft skills gap." Applicants have the right degrees or certs but lack communication or leadership abilities.

This means **abundant opportunities for those who do cultivate these human skills**. It might be why we're seeing a renaissance in soft skills training. LinkedIn Learning reported surging enrollment in courses for creativity, persuasion, and conflict resolution in recent years.

Evidence strongly indicates that doubling down on human skills is a pragmatic career move. The future belongs to those who are both tech-savvy and deeply human-savvy—people who can collaborate with AIs and do what AIs can't. **Creativity, empathy, critical thinking, communication, leadership**—these will never go out of style. They'll only stand out more.

Fast Learning Path: Strengthening Key Human Skills

Creativity and empathy might seem innate. But they are still skills you can practice and develop. Here's how to fast-track growth in these areas.

Creativity–Practice Divergent Thinking

Give yourself a small creative exercise each day. Take a common object or problem. List five alternate uses or solutions for it. Pushing your brain to think beyond the obvious trains it to generate ideas.

Expose yourself to diverse inputs. Read about fields outside your own. Dabble in a creative hobby (sketching, creative writing prompts).

Cross-training your brain fuels creativity in your main work by making you comfortable with free-thinking and associating ideas from different domains.

Empathy–Active Listening Drills

In your next few conversations whether at work or personal, practice fully present listening. Don't interrupt.

1. As you listen, mentally summarize what the other person is expressing, including the emotion behind it.

2. After someone finishes speaking, respond with, "It sounds like you feel X about Y," to ensure you got it. This focuses you on their perspective.

You can also build empathy outside of direct conversations. Research shows that reading fiction or watching films from cultures or experiences different from your own can improve empathy by letting you "live" other lives vicariously.

Critical Thinking—The "5 Whys" Habit

When you encounter a claim, solution, or AI output, practice the "5 Whys." Ask *why* five times. Why is this true? Why is this recommended? Dig deeper each time.

If an AI report says "Increase social media ads," ask: Why will that help? (Perhaps more reach.) Why do we need more reach? (Sales are down.) Why are sales down? (Maybe product awareness is low.) Keep going.

This will train you *not* to take things at face value, to seek root causes and hidden assumptions. Also, seek out opposing viewpoints on issues you feel strongly about. Try to argue from sides you disagree with. This classic debate exercise sharpens your ability to analyze logic and evidence objectively, reducing bias.

Communication—Mirror and Clarity Exercises

To improve interpersonal communication, practice "mirroring" and clear articulation. Mirroring means adopting a similar tone or energy as the person you're communicating with, while staying authentic, to build rapport.

For clarity, challenge yourself to explain a complex aspect of your work in a two-minute "elevator pitch" with no jargon, as if speaking to a friend outside your field. Record yourself and play it back or explain it to a friend and see if they get it.

Do this regularly—pick a concept a week. It will hone your ability to distill and convey ideas clearly. These are essential human skills, especially when working with people and AI outputs.

Leadership & Collaboration—Team Initiative

Even if not in a formal leadership role, find ways to exercise leadership or team-building skills each week. Facilitate part of a meeting. Organize a quick knowledge-share session among colleagues. Offer to mentor a new hire in an area you know well.

These actions develop your ability to guide, support, and influence others—skills AIs don't have. Reflection helps too. After any group project, reflect or journal on team dynamics that went well and what could be improved. This reflection can make you more attuned to group needs and interpersonal strategies next time.

Do This Now: Sharpen Your Human Edge

Spot the Human Moment

Today or tomorrow, identify one interaction or task where you can inject human skill when it might otherwise be lacking.

When you respond to a customer or colleague's email, add an extra sentence showing understanding. For example "I realize this issue has been frustrating for you, and I'm doing my best to resolve it."

In your next team meeting, ask a quiet team member for their opinion— showing inclusion and listening. This immediate action to infuse empathy or attentiveness will improve that outcome. Your habit of leveraging human touch points will grow stronger.

Creative Brainstorm

Take a current challenge you're facing at work or in a personal project. Do a quick 10-minute brainstorm on paper with the rule "no idea is too silly."

Push for at least 10 ideas or approaches, no matter how out-there. If you need to improve team communication, wild ideas might include "all meetings in song" or "daily meme group-chat."

You likely won't do those, but within the absurdity might lie a seed, maybe a daily fun check-in. Choose one promising creative idea from your list—even if it's a little unconventional.

Commit to try it out in practice or at least to pitch it to someone who can help. This exercise flexes your creativity. It shows you there's often more than one "normal" solution to any problem.

Micro "User Manual" for a Colleague

Pick a colleague or client you interact with regularly. Spend a few minutes writing down what you know about how they operate or feel.

Essentially, make a mini "user manual" for that person. What motivates them? What are their pet peeves? How do they prefer to communicate? Long emails, quick calls?

Based on this, identify one adjustment you can make in your interaction to better align with their style or needs. If a client gets overwhelmed by data, prepare a simple visual for your next update to them.

Implement this adjustment in your next interaction. This practices empathy and communication and can tangibly improve relationship and outcomes with that person.

Fact-Check Something by Hand

Today, take one piece of information you'd normally take for granted—something you read in a report or output from a tool. Now verify it using a human approach.

Check the source of a statistic, cross-check a calculation with a quick manual version, or ask for a colleague's perspective on an assumption.

This keeps your critical thinking sharp and reminds you that AI should be checked, not blindly trusted.

Fact Bombs: Human Skills

Skills on the Rise

Surveyed employers project that by 2027, the fastest-growing skills will be predominantly *human*. **Creative thinking ranks #2** in importance. And resilience, flexibility, and agility are among the top five, reflecting the need for workers who can adapt and innovate in disrupted workplaces (WEF, 2023). Likewise, **curiosity and lifelong learning** (drive to grow and adapt) are some of the fastest growing workforce development priorities.

Automation's Upside for Soft Skills

As automation advances, demand for social-emotional and higher cognitive skills accelerates. McKinsey (2018) forecasted **26% growth in demand for social/emotional skills** (like empathy, leadership) and **19% growth for higher cognitive skills** (creativity, critical thinking) in the U.S. by 2030. These human skills are where machines can't easily tread, making them the growth areas for human work.

Soft Skills, Hard Results

Research shows these drive measurable ROI in revenue, retention, and innovation. Teams led by managers with high emotional intelligence (empathy, communication) outperform others in productivity and retention. Companies with strong creative and collaborative cultures (human skills) are **3.5X more likely to outperform their peers in revenue growth** (McKinsey, 2018). Human skills don't just feel nice. They drive innovation, customer satisfaction, and bottom lines in measurable ways.

Chapter 9
Step 6
Build Your Brand and Network

Jamal was a competent engineer with a solid work history. But for years he felt invisible in his industry. Colleagues with similar skills got plucked for new opportunities, promotions, and speaking gigs while he stayed in the same role.

Jamal realized he'd been expecting his work to speak for itself. But in the modern world, **you must speak for your work**.

He decided to actively build his professional brand and network. He started by updating his LinkedIn profile and sharing occasional posts about projects he was excited about. He reached out to old college friends and coworkers to reconnect and talk shop. He began attending a local tech meetup once a month.

Despite being naturally introverted, he pushed himself to meet new people and follow up with them online. Slowly, things changed.

A post he wrote about solving a tricky engineering problem went semi-viral in his company, earning him praise from his VP. A former classmate referred him to a role on an exciting new team. Recruiters began reaching out, instead of him sending out cold applications that went nowhere. In team meetings, higher-ups asked his opinion, since his name having popped up in industry discussions.

By becoming visible and cultivating genuine relationships, Jamal transformed from an unnoticed worker bee into well-connected professional with a reputation. His opportunities exploded because he invested time in his brand and network.

Why It Matters

Building your personal brand and network is like **career insurance, plus a force multiplier** for every other skill you have. Maybe you do excellent work. But if nobody knows about it outside your immediate circle, you'll miss opportunities. Visibility is key. When people think of that skill or area, your name should come to mind. This way, you'll attract opportunities rather than always chasing them.

A strong professional brand, how you present yourself and the value you offer, makes you stand out in a crowded job market. This matters even if you're happily employed. It could lead to a tap for a promotion, invitations to contribute to high-profile projects, or being headhunted for a dream role.

Networking, on the other hand, is the support scaffolding for your entire career. Most jobs and business opportunities come through connections. Up to 80% of jobs are filled through networking rather than cold applications (University of Maryland, Baltimore County, n.d.).

People prefer to work with and recommend those they trust. Cultivating relationships can open doors no amount of blind resume-sending can. A strong network is more than a path to jobs. It's a source of learning, mentorship, collaboration, and resilience. The people you connect with can catch you when you fall and cheer you when you rise.

In the age of LinkedIn and social media, **your "brand" extends online and works 24/7**. Recruiters or potential clients form impressions of you from your online presence, before ever speaking to you.

Being intentional about that presence matters across industries—not just among extroverts or "influencers" but for everyone who wants a sustainable career. Inclusive **networking across genders, cultures, and industries broadens your perspective**, making you more adaptable, and diverse networks foster innovation.

When you build your brand and network, you amplify your other efforts. You might upskill furiously (Step 2) and develop human skills (Step 5). But without visibility and connections, those improvements stay under a rock.

This step ensures your growth is known, your reputation is positive and clear, and you have **allies to help you seize opportunities**, fast-forwarding your career progression.

Evidence & Examples

As we have seen, **most jobs are found through networking**. Figures commonly quoted range from 60% to 85% (Careers in Government, 2024). The U.S. Bureau of Labor, for instance, reported that **70% of jobs are secured through personal and professional connections, not job boards**.

Whatever the exact percentage, many opportunities never make it to public postings. These are filled by referrals and word-of-mouth. One well-known LinkedIn survey found that employees hired via referral tend to have higher job satisfaction and stay longer.

No wonder companies often prefer networking-based hires. If you're *not* networking, you're possibly seeing only a thin slice of available opportunities.

On the personal brand side, consider the role of LinkedIn and social media in recruitment today. In one study, over **95% of recruiters reported using LinkedIn regularly** to find or vet candidates. And most had *rejected* candidates based on online information, from unprofessional posts to inconsistencies in their story (NGPF, n.d.).

The flip side is a strong online presence can make you *more* attractive. Candidates who actively showcase their work, share insights, or have endorsements are seen as more credible and passionate.

According to LinkedIn's analytics, having a profile photo makes you 14 times more likely to be viewed. Having five or more skills listed makes you 33 times more likely to be messaged by recruiters (NGPF, n.d.). These numbers indicate that a polished, complete online brand dramatically increases visibility.

Networking has measurable benefits for career growth and salary. A study by Harvard Business Review found people with rich, open networks (contacts across different groups, not just teammates or family) were **3 times more innovative** than people with small, closed networks. They also tended to get promoted faster.

An analysis by PayScale found that employees who found their job through networking had higher median salaries than those who applied cold. This suggests that referrals can land you better positions or pay. Referred jobs can be higher-quality matches or bypass entry-level gating. In a survey by consulting firm Challenger, Gray & Christmas, **80% of participating executives said networking played a crucial role in their career advancement**.

Real life stories illustrate the power of networks. Think of entrepreneurs. It's often said, investors bet on people as much as ideas. A founder with a strong personal brand and network finds it easier to get meetings, attract talent, and close deals.

Or consider contracting/freelance work. Many freelancers get most gigs through past clients and referrals. If you have a robust network, one project naturally begets the next. Without one, you're constantly marketing yourself from scratch.

There are plenty of personal brand success stories as well. For instance, a young data analyst started sharing cool visualizations and analysis tidbits on LinkedIn and Twitter. She wasn't a manager or a famous expert, just someone consistently putting out valuable insights in her niche.

Over a year, she built a following, got invited to speak at a small conference, and eventually landed a job offer from a company that noticed her posts. This job that was never formally posted anywhere. Essentially, by showcasing her expertise and passion publicly, she attracted an opportunity to herself.

This story repeats in many forms: the engineer who creates a useful open-source tool and gets recruited by a tech giant, or the marketer who posts thoughtful articles and gets consulting inquiries inbound.

Networking goes far beyond job hunting. It drives ongoing growth and innovation. Inside companies, 'learning networks'–employees who connect across departments–

often discover new processes or spark fresh ideas by blending their expertise.

Companies like 3M and Google are famous for encouraging employees to network internally, because cross-team connections often lead to breakthroughs. Externally, a wide network ensures that when you hit a challenge, you don't have to solve it alone—you can call on experts in your circle for guidance.

A cybersecurity specialist recounted how a quick message to an industry Slack channel saved her team days of work. They were able to quickly learn how others solved a specific technical issue. That kind of fast help only happens if you build those relationships.

Another angle: "visibility" within your organization is crucial for promotion. Research found workers who shared their wins and sought visibility—presenting at meetings, volunteering for cross-team projects—were promoted faster than those who did good work quietly.

Managers can't always see everything. A bit of professional visibility ensures your contributions aren't overlooked. When companies undergo layoffs or restructuring, employees with stronger networks, internally and externally, tend to bounce back faster. They are either saved due to their known value or find new roles through contacts.

Effects of networking can be quantified in terms of "reduced search time." Job seekers who network tend to find new positions faster than those who rely solely on online applications.

It might take dozens of online submissions to get one response. But one warm introduction can lead to an interview immediately. This can save months of job hunting and lost income.

And branding doesn't mean you have to be "Insta-famous" or have thousands of followers. You can simply become the "go-to person" for a subject in your local professional circle or within your company.

If colleagues frequently say, "Oh, ask Priya, she knows all about X," you already have a strong brand. Expand that reputation outward. Write a short article or speak on a panel. Amplify it beyond people who know you personally.

In a survey by ExecuNet, **87% of participating recruiters said positive online personal brands influence hiring decisions**. In a CareerBuilder survey, 50% of participating employers won't interview potential hires they can't find online or who have poor/inappropriate online presence.

The evidence is overwhelming. Networking and personal branding are not optional nice-to-haves. They're critical components of a thriving career. They significantly improve your access to opportunities, your professional growth, and even job security.

Brand hygiene is a must in 2025. Make sure your digital footprint is positive and professional. Build your network and brand, and watch good things follow.

Fast Learning Path: Expanding Your Network and Visibility

Building a brand and network takes time. The good news? You don't need giant leaps—you can speed results by starting with small, consistent steps.

Optimize Your Online Profile

For a quick win, update your LinkedIn (or relevant platform) *this week*. Use a professional-looking photo. Write a concise but compelling summary that highlights your unique strengths or accomplishments. List key skills (at least five) and projects.

If someone lands on your profile, they should immediately grasp who you are and what you're good at. Add one or two recent achievements or courses to show you're active and growing. This effort will significantly boost your professional image and start drawing more views (NGPF, n.d.).

Reconnect With 2 People

Think of two former colleagues, classmates, or acquaintances you haven't spoken to in a while, who you respect or just enjoyed talking to. This week, shoot each of them a short message or email.

It can be as simple as "Hey, we haven't caught up in a long time. How are you and what are you working on these days?" Or mention something that reminded you of them.

No agenda, just a genuine reconnection. Small reach-outs often rekindle relationships and can lead to idea-sparking ideas, knowledge, or opportunities. Make it a goal to do this kind of check-in with at least one person every week.

Attend One Event or Join One Group

Find a professional meetup, webinar, or online community related to your field or interests. Commit to attending or participating this month. Introduce yourself to at least one person or contribute one post/comment to introduce yourself and add value. Join a relevant LinkedIn or Facebook group and answer someone's question. Attend a virtual panel and ask a thoughtful question. This gradually expands your network and gets your name out there.

Share Something Small but Valuable

Build your personal brand through content, even in a modest way. In the next two weeks, share a short post on your preferred platform about something professional: a lesson learned, your take on a news article, a shout-out on a colleague's achievement.

You might feel uncomfortable at first, but don't. It's offering value or insight, not bragging. For instance: "Just finished a project optimizing our database. Learned a ton about indexing. If anyone's tackling something similar, happy to share tips!"

This shows you are engaged. And it could prompt interactions from others (networking in action). Aim to post or share like this monthly or more to start, so your profile isn't dormant.

Volunteer or Collaborate

Look for ways to network and build your brand by stepping outside your usual role. Volunteer for a cross-team initiative at work, join a professional project, contribute to open source, or help organize an industry event. Identify one opportunity where you can lend a hand beyond your immediate duties.

It could be as simple as saying, "I saw the marketing team is doing a webinar. I have some data that might help. Should I connect with them?" Or you might volunteer an hour a week at a professional association.

These small actions expand your network by connecting you with new people, while also building your brand as someone who contributes beyond their role.

Do This Now: Boost Your Network & Brand Today

Send Two Messages (Networking Nudge)

Today, reach out to two individuals in your professional orbit. One should be a *strong tie*. It could be someone you know well but haven't talked to recently, a former colleague or mentor. The other should be a *weak tie*, an acquaintance or someone you met at a conference.

- For the strong tie: send a personal catch-up note. "I'd love to hear how you've been since we last worked together."
- For the weak tie: remind them how you met or what you have in common. Express interest in what they're doing. "I recall you were pivoting to UX design—how's that going?"

These small actions maintain and refresh your network. Do it genuinely, with no immediate favor to ask. They might respond with helpful info. At minimum, you've put yourself back on their radar in a friendly way.

Post or Share One Thing (Visibility Nudge)

Take a few minutes to share something work-related on your chosen professional platform. It could be an article you found insightful with a comment from you, or a quick win from work. ("Proud our team just shipped XYZ after months of hard work!") Or share a book/podcast in your field. Be professional and positive in tone. Hit publish.

Immediate action puts a signal out into your network and beyond. It shows you're engaged in your profession. Even if it doesn't get tons of reactions, some people will notice (including lurking recruiters or managers). The key is building a habit of visibility.

Pro Tip: Use AI to polish your post or suggest keywords. For example, paste your draft into an AI tool and ask, "Rewrite this for LinkedIn in a professional but approachable tone."

Update Your Email Signature or Bio

A quick brand builder is to update your email signature, forum bios, or Slack profile at work. Include more of your title—maybe a line about your specialty or a link to your LinkedIn/portfolio, for example, "Jane Doe– Project Manager | Passionate about sustainable design | linkedin.com/in/janedoe." This passively promotes your brand every time you communicate via email, subtly reinforcing what you're about.

Schedule a "Networking Hour"

Block one hour in the next week or two for networking tasks. During that hour, do things like comment on colleagues' posts (supporting others is part of networking), send network nudges, or research local events to attend.

Add this this to your calendar, treat it as a meeting with your future self. Network seriously, like any other work task. Blocking the time makes it much more likely you'll follow through.

Fact Bombs: Networking & Brand

Hidden Job Market

Some **70-80% of jobs are never publicly advertised**. They're filled through internal hires or referrals (University of Maryland, Baltimore County, n.d.). Tapping into this via networking greatly improves your odds of finding positions you want. The *best* opportunities often go to those who know someone on the inside.

Network = Shorter Job Hunt

People who network during job searches tend to land jobs faster. Referrals have a **50-100% higher chance of getting an interview and offer** compared to cold applicants. Workers hired through referral also get in quicker and can have higher starting salaries (on average 6% more) due to trust and endorsement. Networking can pay off in time and money.

LinkedIn Impact

A strong online presence boosts your reach. Having **5+ skills listed on LinkedIn makes you 27 times more likely to appear in recruiter searches**. And profiles with a photo and summary are more likely to get messaged (NGPF, n.d.).

Of recruiters surveyed, **87%** report checking candidates' LinkedIn or social media (NGPF, n.d.). Nearly half have rejected candidates with little or negative social media presence.

Building a positive personal brand online isn't vanity. It's a baseline expectation and can be a deciding factor in getting contacted for opportunities.

Chapter 10
Step 7
Career Agility

Asha began her career as a print journalist. When the news industry went digital, she taught herself web design to help build her newspaper's first website. A decade later, social media emerged. Asha pivoted again, becoming one of the paper's first social media editors, translating traditional reporting into tweets and posts.

In her 40s, she took an interest in data journalism. She learned basic coding and reinvented herself once more. She became a data reporter who could crunch numbers for investigative stories. Now in her 50s, Asha leads a digital content strategy team, thriving in an industry that's unrecognizable compared to when she started.

Her secret? **Career agility**–the willingness to pivot, re-skill, and chase new opportunities rather than clinging to an old identity. While others resisted change or feared starting over, Asha embraced it as a continuous adventure.

She has lived multiple "career lives"–reporter, designer, editor, analyst, strategist–all in one journey. Each reinvention builds on the last. And she's never been left behind by the currents of change. Asha's story proves that career agility isn't about instability. It's about **staying in motion so you're always where growth is happening**.

Why It Matters

Career agility means having the ability to pivot and reinvent yourself as industries, roles, and entire markets change. It is the cornerstone skill in the age of AI and constant disruption–the mindset and flexibility to navigate shifts and adapt in your work life. This matters more than ever. The era of linear, one-field, 30-year careers with a single company is largely gone.

Technology changes, industries rise and fall, and interests evolve. Career agility means not tying your identity to a single job title. Instead, you see your transferable core skills and experience as tools ready to be applied in new ways. This perspective is vital for staying employed and fulfilled over a lifetime.

Studies suggest that new generations may have dozens of roles and several distinct careers across their working lives. Many of tomorrow's jobs don't even exist yet. Career agility prepares you to step into those roles when they appear, guarding against stagnation.

Agile professionals are often first to spot emerging opportunities. They move toward growing areas while others stay stuck in shrinking ones. When disruption hits—sudden layoffs or downturns—those with agility bounce back faster because they pivot into fresh directions.

On a personal level, career agility keeps you engaged and prevents burnout. New challenges can reignite motivation and fuel continual growth. Employers value agility too. They actively seek people with diverse experiences and fresh perspectives.

For organizations, agile employees are priceless because they can shift roles as circumstances change. For individuals, career agility transforms uncertainty from something to fear into something to embrace. It gives you the confidence to adapt, pivot, and seize new possibilities.

Be proactive, not reactive. Think of your career as a dynamic startup that you continuously iterate and pivot to meet market demands. You remain the author of your career story, not just a character swept along by outside forces.

Evidence & Examples

Workforce trends highlight why career agility matters. The median job tenure today is only about four years (USA Facts, 2024), and it's even shorter for younger workers. People are no longer sticking with one employer or even one career track. A landmark study found those born in the late 1950s and early 1960s held 12 jobs by age 50, and newer generations—facing faster industry shifts—are on track for even more.

"Career pivoting" is becoming a normalized concept. According to polls, most working professionals anticipate at least one significant career change. LinkedIn data indicates a rising number of members who have worked across *multiple* industries. People don't seem to be staying in single domains. In one analysis, LinkedIn reported a 50% increase in people who switch fields in a five-year span. Switching tracks is now increasingly common.

Agility is also needed in terms of job role mutation. Think "SEO specialist" or "UI/UX designer." These scarcely existed 15 years ago. Now they're mainstream. According to the World Economic Forum, some **65% of children entering primary school today will be working in job types that don't exist** (WEF, 2023).

The point is new roles pop up as technology and needs evolve, for example, "AI ethicist" or "drone traffic manager" could be in high demand in the near future. People already in the workforce must be agile to hop into new roles as they arise.

Agility is also about internal moves. Companies like IBM famously encourage employees to "reboot" their careers internally. They reported major movement of staff into new roles through retraining. On a broad scale, an **average of 44% of surveyed workers anticipate their skills disrupted** in five years (WEF, 2023).

World Economic Forum explicitly recommends continuous, career-long learning and agility as the answer to the rapid skill churn. On a macro level, McKinsey projects that up to **14% of the global workforce may need to switch occupations by 2030** (Fennell, 2025) due to AI/automation. This suggests that millions will need to pivot, not just learn one new skill for the same job.

Consider real-world examples. The COVID-19 pandemic forced massive career agility in a short span. People in hospitality or aviation, for instance, suddenly had to rethink their careers when those sectors collapsed temporarily.

Success stories emerged. Restaurant managers pivoted into project management in other industries by emphasizing their operations and people-management skills. Flight attendants moved into customer success for software companies, drawing on communication and service skills.

Those who rebranded their skills for new contexts landed on their feet. Those who didn't remain stuck as their industry struggled.

Another example. Some Blockbuster video store managers in the 2000s anticipated streaming and shifted into other retail or went back to school for IT. Those folks likely continued fine. Those who didn't pivot faced a dead end when the stores closed.

Similarly, consider technology workers. Hot programming languages or frameworks might be obsolete in 5-10 years, for example, Flash developers had to completely retrain when Flash was phased out.

The agile continuously learn new languages and even change specializations, for example, from web developer to mobile developer to data engineer over a career. Career agility correlates with entrepreneurial activities. Many agile professionals start side hustles or businesses—not necessarily to become billionaires, but to diversify skills and income.

Side projects and entrepreneurial experiments also reflect agility. Whether or not they become full careers, they build versatility. The larger trend is clear: reskilling is no longer optional. An OECD report projected that by 2025, the average worker would reskill three times in their career due to automation and shifting markets. That level of reinvention demands agility.

Longer careers make agility even more essential. With people often working into their 70s, a career can now span nearly 50 years. The half-life of skills, however, is shrinking—what you learned in your 20s may be obsolete by your 60s. Agility ensures that mid-life transitions or later-life career shifts become smooth reinventions rather than crises.

Companies increasingly look for "learning agility"—ability to rapidly acquire new skills and adapt to new roles—in hiring. In a survey by Korn Ferry, learning agility was found to be a top predictor of leadership success. And high learning-agile individuals were promoted twice as fast. They were also considered more likely to succeed in new roles because they quickly pivot in their duties or approach as needed.

One inspiring example comes from the 2010s, when IBM retrained tens of thousands of workers as older roles, such as mainframe operators, declined and new ones, like cloud computing specialists, emerged. Employees had to embrace career agility—learning new technologies and sometimes moving into different departments. Those who adapted not only kept their jobs but often stepped into cutting-edge roles.

Many of us will face moments when our industry or profession is hit by change (tech-driven, economic, or even a pandemic). Agility transforms such moments from catastrophes into possible springboards. It might mean going back to school at 35 or 50, which evidence shows is increasingly happening. Mid-career folks are enrolling in bootcamps, MBAs, certifications, etc., to change direction.

Data from platforms like Coursera show that many of their learners are mid-career people reskilling or upskilling, not just college kids. The evidence is overwhelming: modern careers are zig-zags, not straight lines. Comfort with pivots and reinvention isn't optional—it's the key to thriving as the world changes around us.

Those who cultivate agility often have the most interesting career stories. And they remain relevant and satisfied even as the world changes around them.

Fast Learning Path: Cultivating Career Agility

Becoming more agile in your career starts with mindset and small strategic behaviors. Here's how to get on the fast track.

Adopt a Growth Portfolio Mindset

Think of your career as an investment portfolio of skills and experiences you're constantly balancing and updating. List your core skills and emerging skills you'd like to acquire. Aim to "invest" time in at least one new skill every year.

By viewing your skills as fluid assets, you won't cling to one identity. ("I'm only a marketer.") You see yourself as a versatile professional who can deploy different skills as needed.

As an exercise, write down *three alternative career paths* you could take with additional learning. For example, with your people skills, consider HR. Or with your hobbyist coding, consider technology. This exercise keeps your mind open to possibilities and highlights areas to develop.

Scan the Horizon Regularly

Periodically review trends in your industry and adjacent fields. Every few months, spend an hour with credible reports or trusted voices to see where things are heading.

Ask Yourself:

- Which new roles are emerging?
- Which skills are losing relevance?

Don't be the last to spot a shift. Set up Google Alerts and subscribe to a future-of-work newsletter relevant to your field.

Being informed early is half the battle. It gives you time to pivot or prepare. For instance, if you notice more talk about AI in your field, consider dabbling with those tools proactively.

Embrace Stretch Assignments and Lateral Moves

Don't wait for the perfect moment to pivot. Use your current job as a lab. Volunteer for tasks or projects outside your usual expertise ("stretch assignments").

If your company has internal openings or rotation programs, consider a lateral move to a different team or function, even if it's a sideways step. It might feel like starting over in some ways. But it builds your adaptability muscle. If you're in finance, try a stint in operations.

Changing environments within a company can be a safe way to experience a pivot. It quickly brings you up to speed in a new area while you are still in a familiar organization. Plus, employers love seeing diverse experience on a resume.

Keep an Exit Strategy (or Three)

Always have a Plan B (and C). This doesn't mean being disloyal. It means you're prepared. Update your resume at least twice a year with new accomplishments. And keep a running list of roles or companies that interest you.

Also, maintain some savings or emergency funds if possible. Financial cushioning buys agility because you can take a calculated risk such as learning something new or enduring a short job gap without panic.

Psychological trick. Imagine if your current job/industry disappeared next year. What would you do? Thinking this way from time to time can reduce fears and prime you to act swiftly if needed. It's easier to pivot if you've mentally rehearsed it.

Rebrand Yourself Gradually

If you aspire to pivot into a new domain, start rebranding before the full jump. Tweak how you present yourself.

If you're a teacher wanting to go into UX design, mention your design projects or user empathy skills in conversations and online profiles. Take on a freelance project. Get certification in that area and add it to your credentials. When you formally go for a UX job, people will already associate you with UX experience.

Don't be pigeonholed by your past title. Use small shifts to signal your new direction. Post content about the new field and join related communities. Highlight your transferable skills, and over a few months continuously shift outsiders' perception of you. This will make your eventual pivot smoother, since your professional brand will have evolved to support it.

Do This Now: Boost Your Agility Today

Learn One "Mini-skill" Outside Your Comfort Zone

Pick a small skill or tool adjacent to your current role but not part of it. Spend an hour learning it, today or this week. If you're a marketer, learn a bit of HTML. If you're a programmer, learn a bit about UI design principles. If you're a nurse, learn a few medical phrases in Spanish.

You won't master it in an hour, but you'll break the ice. The act of starting to learn a new skill is a micro-pivot that builds confidence for bigger changes. It can spark interest in pursuing it further. At worst, you gain knowledge. At best, you discover a new direction.

Refresh Your Resume with a Future Lens

Take 30 minutes to update your resume *not just with what you've done, but also in terms of what you want to do next*. Add any recently acquired skills, certifications, or relevant side projects. Also ask, does this resume position me for future roles? If not, tweak the language to be more forward-compatible.

If you've mostly done print design but want to move digital, emphasize any digital-related tasks you've handled, even if minor, and maybe downplay the word "print." Doing this now ensures that if opportunity arises or you need to job search suddenly, you'll project agility and readiness for what's next.

Reach out to someone in a field you're curious about. Identify a person, perhaps a LinkedIn connection or friend-of-a-friend who works in a role or industry you'd consider pivoting to someday. Send a polite note asking for a 20-minute chat to learn about what they do—essentially an informational interview.

Do it now. Most people enjoy talking about themselves and helping others. The worst that can happen is they're busy. Having that conversation, even via email, will give you insights into that field. And you'll have a possible contact there, making the potential pivot less abstract and more tangible.

You might discover it's more or less glamorous or exciting than you thought—either way, you gain clarity.

Do a Career "Pre-mortem"

Take a moment today for a thought experiment. Imagine it's five years from now and you *didn't* adapt to changes. Perhaps your role was automated or your industry had a downturn and you struggled. Now ask, "What likely caused that, and what could I have done to avoid it?" This pre-mortem exercise can be motivating.

It might highlight, for example, "I saw AI coming but ignored it." Or "I stayed in a declining sector without adding new skills." Those become action items for now. Write down two things from this exercise that you can do to ensure the imagined scenario doesn't happen.

Maybe it's "keep building data skills" or "expand network in growth industries." By doing this now, you help future-proof yourself. You address potential regrets in advance—a hallmark of agility—and eliminate them.

Fact Bombs: Career Agility

Job Switching is Standard

The average U.S. worker now changes jobs roughly every **four years** (even less for younger workers) (USA Facts, 2024). They have about **12 jobs** in their lifetime. This frequency of change shows that shifting roles and careers are the norm, not the exceptions, making adaptability a critical asset.

Occupational Reinvention

Up to **14% of the global workforce** (hundreds of millions of workers) may need to switch to a *different* occupation by 2030. This is due to automation and shifts in labor demand (Fennell, 2025). Entire job categories will shrink while new ones emerge. Career reinvention skills will equal survival for many.

Skills Half-Life & Lifelong Learning

Technical skills can have a "half-life" as short as **five years** (IBM, 2021). Many skills may be half as relevant in five years as they are today. To stay marketable, workers must refresh or replace skills continuously.

By 2025, **50% of all employees were projected to need reskilling** (IBM, 2021). Embracing that reality with an agile mindset (ready to learn new skills and pivot often) is essential. Do it to avoid becoming outdated and seize new opportunities in the ever-evolving job landscape.

Part III

THE NEXT 90 DAYS AND BEYOND

Chapter 11
Your 90-Day Career Change Plan

Workplaces are changing at breakneck speed. During the pandemic alone, career shifts accelerated by 50% (McKinsey Global Institute, 2023). Analysts project disruption to a quarter of today's jobs in the next five years (WEF, 2023).

In this climate, you can't afford to take a backseat. The earlier "Do This Now" actions helped you build momentum with small, focused steps. This chapter builds on that foundation with a structured 90-day roadmap.

We'll break your goals into 30/60/90-day milestones, building robust networking strategies, outlining upskilling pathways, and securing quick wins with minimal cost. By the end, you'll have a clear "Do This Now" action checklist to accelerate your career growth.

30/60/90-Day Roadmap

Plan in Sprints. Think of the next three months as three 30-day sprints, each with specific objectives that ladder up to your bigger career goal. Breaking up your plan creates urgency and allows for quick wins and course-corrections. Use AI tools to help map out your milestones, track progress, and adjust your plan as new opportunities arise.

Roles are evolving rapidly. Employers are redesigning jobs, and 40% of core skills are expected to shift due to automation (IBM, 2024). A short-cycle plan helps you make tangible progress before the landscape changes again.

Days 1-30 Set Your Foundation

Use this month to clarify your career target and gather insights. Define a 90-day goal, for example, "land a data analytics project" or "acquire X certification." Outline the steps to get there. Research the skills and qualifications in demand for your desired role by reviewing job postings and talking to people in that field. AI tools can speed this up by analyzing job ads, summarizing role requirements, and highlighting the most in-demand skills for you.

Identify 5 to 10 people in your network or industry to connect with for advice or mentorship. Use AI to draft tailored outreach messages, making it easier to break the ice and start meaningful conversations.

Tip. Keep this phase lean and learning-focused. By day 30, you should have a concrete goal, a list of skills to develop, and a schedule for networking and learning.

Days 31-60 Build and Engage

In month two, intensify your actions. Work on the skill gaps you identified and dedicate time each week to practice. Use AI tools to create custom quizzes, generate sample projects, or suggest exercises so your learning sticks. Remember, many employers predict 30% or more of tasks could be automated by 2030 (McKinsey Global Institute, 2023)—so upskilling is non-negotiable.

Ramp up networking too. Reach out to contacts for informational interviews and use AI to prepare smart questions or draft tailored outreach notes. Attend at least one professional event, virtually or in person, and let AI help you summarize and reflect on what you learn.

Start sharing your progress more publicly. AI can help you polish a LinkedIn post or transform a project into a short case study to showcase your growing expertise.

Aim to apply new skills in small but visible ways during this period. Automate a simple task at work with a new software tool, contribute to an open-source project, or share an AI-assisted case study. By day 60, you should have tangible progress: new connections made, skills applied in real projects, and growing confidence.

Days 61-90 Execute and Leverage Quick Wins

In this third sprint, focus on tangible outcomes that demonstrate your growth. Update your resume and LinkedIn if you're considering external moves, or update your internal portfolio and performance tracker if you're aiming for growth within your current role.

Actively look for opportunities to apply your enhanced skill set:

- If job hunting: apply for a stretch role, pitch a freelance project, or start interviewing.
- If staying in your role: propose a new initiative, volunteer for a high-visibility project, or mentor a colleague using your new skills.

Leverage your network. If you're exploring external options, follow up with contacts and ask about leads. If you're building internally, connect with cross-functional peers, join company resource groups, or set up conversations with senior leaders to showcase your new capabilities.

Remember, visibility is key. Around 80% of opportunities are filled through personal connections and referrals (New York State Department of Labor, 2024). That applies just as much inside organizations as in the open job market.

By Day 90, aim to achieve a significant milestone. For some, that may be completing a certification, securing an interview, or launching a portfolio website. For others, it may be presenting a project at a team meeting, getting leadership buy-in for a new initiative, or building credibility as the "go-to" person in your area of growth. Choose an achievement that visibly propels you closer to your next level.

Stay Agile

Treat this 90-day roadmap as a living plan. At the end of each sprint, review your progress using these prompts:

- What worked well this month?
- What slowed me down?
- What new skills or knowledge did I gain?
- Which activities gave me energy? Which drained me?
- Who did I connect with?
- How did it expand my network or visibility?
- What new opportunities or insights surfaced?
- What adjustments will I make for the next sprint?

Use AI to summarize your notes into strengths, gaps, and opportunities; generate tailored prompts for your role; and draft an action plan for your next sprint.

These reflections give you the insight to adapt your plan, so each sprint builds on real progress instead of guesswork.

The ability to pivot is a strength in an AI-driven job market that's already moving fast (McKinsey Global Institute, 2023). If new information or opportunities emerge such as a sudden demand for your new skill, a contact opening a door for you, adjust your plan to leverage it. Remember, action beats perfection. A critical step is to generate momentum in these 90 days. Even modest progress builds confidence and lays a foundation for longer-term moves.

Networking Strategy

No matter how high-tech the world becomes, *who* you know can be as important as *what* you know. An effective networking strategy is critical to accelerate your career. Opportunities often flow through people.

Most jobs are found through networking rather than cold applications (New York State Department of Labor, 2024). Your next big break might come from a conversation, not a job board.

Quality Over Quantity

Build a *strong* professional network, not just a large one. Identify peers, mentors, and influencers in your industry or target field. Reach out with genuine curiosity and a giving mindset. Networking is about building relationships, not just asking for favors.

Share a useful article or congratulate a contact on a recent accomplishment before diving into career talk. Referrals carry weight because they come with trust. Contacts only recommend people they deem serious and reliable (Vilorio, 2011). Work on establishing trust over time.

Leverage Multiple Channels

In the AI era, networking happens both in-person and online. Use professional social platforms such as LinkedIn, to connect with colleagues, alumni, and thought leaders. Join online communities or forums related to your interests whether it's a data science Slack group or an industry association's discussion board. And don't neglect traditional networking. Attend webinars, conferences, or local meetups where you can interact face-to-face or in real time. A balanced approach can expand your reach.

Be Clear In Your Purpose

When engaging your network, communicate your goals and ask targeted questions.

Instead of a generic "let me know if you hear of any jobs," try "I'm transitioning into UX design and recently earned a certification. I'd love your insight on which companies are innovating in this space."

This invites specific help or information. As your 90-day plan progresses, update mentors on your wins. People are more inclined to help when they see you taking initiative and making progress.

Two-Way Benefit Is Key

Give back. Offer help to others in your network. Things like sharing a job posting, providing a reference, or offering encouragement on projects can go far. Building goodwill makes networking a two-way street and strengthens your professional relationships.

Over the long run, supportive networks become invaluable career assets. They can alert you to opportunities early, vouch for your skills, and even partner with you on new ventures.

Cultivate them with care and consistency.

Networking Quick Tips

- **Set weekly outreach goals**. For example, send two catch-up messages to former colleagues and one introductory message to a new contact each week. Regular, small steps lead to strong ties.

- **Use the "give before you take" rule.** Whenever you meet someone new, think of something of value you can share—insights, resources, offer of help—before asking for anything.

- **Update your online presence.** Ensure your LinkedIn (or equivalent) reflects your latest skills and projects. Post or comment about topics in your field to become visible to your network for the right reasons.

- **Follow up and stay in touch.** After any networking interaction including a coffee chat, event, or online exchange, send a thank-you or follow-up note. Down the line, periodically check in. Genuine, periodic touchpoints keep relationships alive.

Upskilling Pathways

In a world where technology and best practices evolve rapidly, continuous upskilling is your career insurance. The World Economic Forum estimates that about **40% of workers' core skills** will change due to automation and digitization (IBM, 2024). And business leaders echo the need for reskilling (IBM, 2024).

The takeaway. Everyone, from new graduates to seasoned professionals, must keep learning to stay relevant. The good news is that upskilling has never been more accessible.

Identify Your Learning Targets

Start by pinpointing skills with the biggest impact on your goals. If your field is being touched by AI, improve your technology literacy. Learn data analysis, basic programming, or relevant AI tools.

And don't ignore uniquely human "power skills" **like communication, attention to detail, and leadership. These remain in high demand** and complement AI's capabilities (WEF, 2025).

Excelling at analyzing data is great. Being able to *communicate* insights and lead a team will make you invaluable. Aim for a blend of domain-specific technical skills and transferable soft skills.

Explore Diverse Learning Pathways

There are more ways to learn now than ever—many of them low-cost or free.

- **Online courses and MOOCs**. Platforms like edX, Coursera, and Khan Academy offer courses from introductory to advanced levels, often free to audit. You can gain certificates in everything from machine learning to project management. These are flexible and self-paced, ideal for evenings or weekends.

- **Certifications and bootcamps**. For more structured or accelerated learning, consider professional certificate programs (a certified data analytics course or a UX design bootcamp). Many are relatively affordable and highly valued by employers (especially in IT, finance, and emerging tech fields).

- **Micro-credentials and digital badges**. Short modules that certify a specific skill (Google's certificates or IBM's digital badges) can be quick wins. They validate your proficiency in a niche (say, "data visualization with Tableau"), enhancing your resume. Employers increasingly recognize these credentials as evidence of practical skills (WEF, 2025).

- **On-the-job training and stretch projects.** The ultimate upskill is experience. Volunteer for a work project that uses a new tool or approach, even outside your comfort zone. Rotational programs, cross-functional teams, or asking to help with a new initiative can provide hands-on learning.

- **Workshops, webinars, and podcasts.** Subscribe to industry webinars or virtual workshops. Many are free and run by experts who share the latest trends. Listen to relevant podcasts during your commute to spark new ideas and keep your knowledge fresh.

Set a regular schedule for learning. Dedicate time for online courses or commit to a personal-growth project. Consistency beats cramming. Consider learning with others. Join a study group or online forum for the skill you're developing—to keep you accountable and exposed to different perspectives.

Leverage employer support. If you're currently employed, see if your organization offers learning benefits—such as sponsored courses, workshops, or internal training. Since 74% of workers prefer to learn through their employer (WEF, 2025), many companies are expanding these opportunities. Using them helps you build new skills while showing your employer you're engaged and valuable.

Finally, embrace lifelong learner mindsets. View upskilling as an ongoing habit. AI era careers have multiple inflection points requiring new skills. The more comfortable you are with spontaneously acquiring knowledge, the more easily you'll navigate those transitions. Lifelong learning isn't a personal enrichment slogan. It's a survival strategy for a fulfilling career (WEF, 2025).

Quick Wins & Low-Cost Options

Career acceleration doesn't always require big investments of time or money. *Small, strategic actions* can yield immediate benefits. This section explores quick wins—things you can do in days or weeks that boost your profile, skills, and opportunities without breaking the bank.

Polish Your Professional Brand

A fast, cost-free win is to update and refine your resume and online profiles. Incorporate your new skills and use clear, results-oriented language to describe your accomplishments. Recruiters often use digital tools to scan for keywords. Make sure your materials reflect the in-demand skills in your field.

This simple update can dramatically increase your visibility for opportunities. Likewise, refresh your LinkedIn headline to something dynamic about what you do or are aiming for (for example, "Marketing Analyst | Data-Driven Storyteller | AI Enthusiast"). A sharp profile can attract connections and job inquiries.

Apply AI Tools To Boost Productivity

Embrace free or freemium technology tools that can amplify your output. Experiment with generative AI assistants (like ChatGPT or other domain-specific AI tools) in brainstorming, research, or streamlining routine tasks. Using AI wisely can free up time for higher-value work.

Learning to work alongside AI is becoming as essential as learning to use the internet was decades ago (IBM, 2024). Showing you can integrate new technology into your workflow is a quick win that signals you're adaptable and efficient.

Grab Free Learning Resources

Identify one *micro-skill* you've been meaning to learn and challenge yourself to complete a short tutorial on it this week. Attend free coding workshops or webinars on leadership skills. Watch YouTube tutorials for problem-solving tips and tricks. Bite-sized learning bursts can have outsized impacts on your competency.

Expand Your Experience Portfolio

If you need to diversify experience but can't switch jobs, consider volunteering or freelancing. Volunteer social media hours for a local nonprofit to hone your digital marketing skills. Help a friend's small business set up an e-commerce site to practice web development.

These efforts cost you time but are concrete projects for your portfolio that expand your network through collaborators. Volunteer projects or gig tasks make your resume pop, showcasing initiative and real-world skills application.

Seek "Quick Win" Assignments

At your current job, identify and solve a problem or improve a process. Speed up manual data entry with a simple spreadsheet macro or draft FAQs to minimize customer support calls.

Curing pain points earns recognition and builds skill credibility. It shows leadership you are proactive and solution-oriented. These mini-projects often require little more than creativity and effort. But they can change how you're perceived in an organization from follower to go-to problem solver.

Quick wins are about being resourceful. They demonstrate that even without an extensive budget or title, you can drive progress. Low-cost wins are building blocks in your career narrative of being agile, value-driven, and continuously improving.

Celebrate small victories. They add up and keep you motivated for bigger goals.

Do This Now: Your Action Plan

Define Your 90-Day Goal

Write down a specific outcome you want to see within three months. Clarity will drive your plan.

Break it into Milestones

Divide your goal into 30-day sub goals. For each, list two to three key actions (such as "Month 1: enroll in course and reconnect with five contacts"). Mark these on your calendar.

Schedule Learning Time

Block out a weekly time slot dedicated to skill-building. Treat it like an important meeting with yourself. Consistency is key to upskilling.

Reach Out to Two People

Identify someone in your current network and one new person in your field to reach out to *this week*. Send a thoughtful message to start a conversation or request a brief call. Networking starts with small steps.

Find a Quick Win

Choose one easy, low-cost, value-adding action you can take in the next two weeks. Sign up for a free webinar. Update one section of your LinkedIn profile. Or solve a minor issue at work. Do it and note the result.

Review and Adjust

Each week, review your progress against your mini-goals. If you're ahead, great. Add a new challenge. If you're behind, identify why, and adapt your plan. Agility will keep you on track.

By executing these steps, you'll set your 90-day accelerator in motion. The journey has begun. Keep up the momentum, stay flexible, and don't forget to acknowledge your progress along the way. Small wins lead to big wins in your next level career.

Chapter 12
The Opportunity Window

There are moments in history when big shifts create narrow but golden windows of opportunity. **Now is such a moment for your career**. The convergence of AI breakthroughs, societal changes, and working practices has opened doors for those ready to step through.

This chapter explores why *today* is the best time to act, drawing parallels to past revolutions to show how seizing the moment pays off. We'll discuss how to spot and grab AI-driven opportunities, position yourself for long-term success, and take immediate action.

Finally, our close will remind you that the AI era can become the launchpad for your greatest career leap.

Why Now Is the Best Time to Act

If you've been waiting for the "right time" to advance or reinvent your career, it's here. Change is not on the horizon. It's all around us, *right now*. Companies are adopting AI and automation on a large scale. Entire industries are reconfiguring, and new roles are emerging.

This flux means opportunity for those prepared to move. Nearly **25% of jobs globally are expected to change significantly in the next five years** (WEF, 2025). Such rapid change is unprecedented. It signals massive demand for new skills and ideas, and chances for agile individuals to step into freshly created voids.

There's also an urgency. Delaying action could mean getting left behind. A recent Gallup poll found that **one in four workers fear their job will become obsolete due to AI** (up from one in seven just a few years prior) (IBM, 2024). Even top HR executives acknowledge that AI will imminently displace certain roles (IBM, 2024).

The sooner you start learning new technologies, adapting to new workflows, and leveraging new tools, the better positioned you'll be. Those who hesitate may find the gap hard to close later. Acting now gives you a competitive edge. During times of talent disruption, employers are often more open-minded about whom to hire or promote.

We're already seeing companies that face skill shortages **hiring for skills and potential rather than strict credentials** to tap into diverse talent pools (McKinsey Global Institute, 2023). Demonstrate the right capabilities—even without a traditional background or degree—and you have a shot. A self-taught coder with a portfolio might land a role that once required a computer science degree, because demand is high.

As of Sept 2025, some **7 million jobs remained unfilled in the U.S.** amidst a labor crunch (Mutikani, 2025; McKinsey Global Institute, 2023). Employers need capable people. And many will train or consider candidates that might've been overlooked in more stable times. This is your chance to shine by showcasing skills, grit, and adaptability.

Finally, consider the *energy* of this moment, the sense of possibility—the buzz—around AI, green energy, biotech and more. New ventures are being funded, pilot projects launched, and bold ideas welcomed. When the world is in flux, **career moves that were risky in steadier times are safer now** because everyone is experimenting.

Now is the time to be proactive. Learn aggressively, network extensively, and volunteer for the future. Windows of opportunity don't stay open forever. But while they are, those who leap can land in extraordinary positions.

Historical Parallels

To understand today, let's look at how bold action during past disruptions changed lives and industries. History doesn't repeat exactly, but it often rhymes.

The AI revolution has been compared to the **Industrial Revolution**, the **rise of the internet**, and other major inflection points.

In each case, those who recognized the opportunity and adapted early reaped huge rewards, while those who resisted or delayed often fell behind.

Industrial Revolution (18th-19th Centuries)

When steam power and mechanization hit the scene, many traditional artisans were put out of work. The famed Luddites even destroyed machines in protest. At the same time, new careers emerged—machine operators, engineers, railroad conductors, factory managers. A farmer's son who learned to operate a steam engine suddenly had a skill set in hot demand, commanding better wages in a growing city industry.

Those who *trained on new machines* or applied their skills to new manufacturing processes found employment and upward mobility as industries boomed (World Economic Forum, 2025). The lesson? Technology may eliminate certain jobs, but it also *creates* new—often better—positions. The key is always to pivot into the new areas being created.

The Internet and Globalization (Late 20th Century)

Fast-forward to the 1990s and early 2000s. The internet went from a niche academic network to a global economic force. Many businesses that failed to embrace the web were left in the dust. Businesses that ignored the web quickly fell behind. Brick-and-mortar retailers couldn't compete with e-commerce, and newspapers that were slow to go online also struggled to survive.

Individuals who jumped into the tech boom—even without a formal technology background—often found astounding success. Self-taught programmers or marketers who grasped SEO could suddenly launch startups or become key hires at dot-com companies.

The digital revolution created millions of jobs, roles like web developer, IT security analyst, digital marketer, etc. exploded in the 2000s. New companies—Google, Amazon, Microsoft, Apple—became giants, offering opportunities for early joiners.

Those who recognized "this internet thing" as the future and educated themselves in it continue to ride that wave to new heights. Globalization too continues to open pathways. Professionals who learn new languages or understand cross-cultural trade are increasingly valued by multinational companies.

Other parallels exist. More recent shifts include the advent of smartphones, the rise of app development and UX design roles, and the expansion of the gig economy. Each wave of innovation—from centralized power stations to personal computing—follows a similar story.

At first, there's uncertainty and fear. "Will this new technology make my job irrelevant?" But soon there's realization of the accompanying new needs and roles. Those who catch on early become pioneers in their fields.

Today's AI-driven transformation is in line with these patterns. We're at the dawn of the **"Fourth Industrial Revolution."** AI, robotics, digital biology, and other emerging fields are blurring boundaries.

New professions are emerging in data science, AI ethics, machine learning engineering, green energy technology, and advanced healthcare (World Economic Forum, 2025). A decade ago, job titles like "cloud architect" or "AI prompt engineer" didn't exist. Now they are highly sought.

The World Economic Forum notes that emerging professions are strongest in five areas: the green economy, data and AI, engineering and cloud computing, product development, and human-centered roles in care, education, and creative fields (WEF, 2025).

As in past revolutions, opportunities crop up directly from new technology (AI developers) and in complementary areas that maintain the human touch (creative content, care jobs, upskill trainers, etc.).

The take-home message from history: **fortune favors the bold—and the prepared**. Each disruptive era has its winners and losers. The winners are not always those with the most resources or status.

Often, they are ordinary people who make extraordinary decisions to adapt and learn. They spot growing needs and position themselves to fill them, willing to let go of old ways and master new tools or concepts.

Spotting and Seizing AI-Driven Opportunities

How do you find opportunities amidst all this change? To start, stay informed and curious, and look for problems that you—armed with new technology and skills—can solve. AI-driven opportunities are arising in most fields, from tech and finance to manufacturing and the arts. Here's how to spot them and make them yours.

Watch Where Investment and Growth Are Headed

A clear indicator of opportunity is where companies are investing money and hiring aggressively. Current data shows huge growth in tech-aligned roles.

For instance, data scientist and information security analyst roles are projected to grow some 36% and 33%, respectively, over the 2020s—leaps far greater than the average job growth rates (US Bureau of Labor Statistics [USBLS], 2025).

Similarly, openings in fields like AI/machine learning, cybersecurity, cloud computing, and renewable energy are seeing massive annual growth. Industry reports and news releases about AI booming in healthcare or record investments in fintech signal opportunity.

Analysts suggest that while some jobs will disappear, **nearly 170 million new jobs may be created in the next five years** driven by technology (like AI) and shifts to a greener economy (WEF, 2025). Such macro trends point to where demand will be. Align your career sails to those winds.

Identify Pain Points and Inefficiencies

Look for ground-level opportunities. In your current job or industry, what are the biggest challenges or inefficiencies? Could AI or new technology help address them?

Maybe you notice that in marketing, analyzing customer data takes forever—an opportunity to introduce AI analytics tools or to specialize in data-driven marketing. Or in education, teachers struggle with individualized lesson plans—an opening for AI-assisted platforms and those who know how to use them.

The first people to apply new technology solutions in a traditionally non-technology field often become trailblazers. If you're in a non-technology role, ask: which parts of my job could be augmented or improved by automation or AI? Then take initiative. Learn the relevant tool or approach. Experiment with a pilot project. Become your team's go-to person for that innovation. **Spot the gap + learn the solution = your opportunity**.

Look At Emerging Roles And Intersections

Scan job boards and professional networks noting the volume of openings and *new titles* or hybrid roles. The job market is fluid right now. Roles like "AI Product Manager," "Automation Coach," or "Data Ethics Officer" are popping up.

Often, these roles seek a mix of skills (for instance, domain expertise + AI familiarity). If you have one half of the combo, consider developing the other. Maybe you're an experienced nurse. The rise of AI in healthcare requires "clinical data analysts" who understand nursing and analytics.

For finance experts, fintech companies increasingly need product leads with both finance and AI expertise. Some of the best opportunities exist at the intersection of fields, where talent is scarce. By developing interdisciplinary skills, you can qualify for cutting-edge roles.

Prepare To Seize—Then Pounce

Spotting an opportunity is useless if you don't act on it. "Seizing" means you may have to step out of your comfort zone. That could be applying for a stretch job, pitching a new role to your employer, or starting a side hustle or business in an unmet niche.

Keep in mind, nearly half (49%) of companies surveyed by the WEF (2023) expect that adopting AI will create new jobs over the coming five years. New tasks and departments will form. Don't be afraid to propose yourself as the person to take on something new.

For example, if your company is dabbling in AI, volunteer to lead or liaise on the project even if it's unofficial. If a startup in your area is growing, reach out and highlight how your skills can help them tackle their challenges.

Action is the bridge between spotting an opportunity and gaining from it.

Ways To Seize An Opportunity You've Spotted

- Dive into a personal project. If you see an opportunity in say, AI-driven app development, start a mini project at home to build a prototype. Experience and results can lead to job offers or business viability.
- Upskill precisely for the role. Once you know the opportunity (for example, data analytics in supply chain management), take a targeted course or gain certification in that area. This equips you and signals your seriousness.
- Network within growth circles. Connect with people already working in emerging areas. Join professional

- groups. Attend meetups or virtual conferences related to it. Often, hearing insiders talk helps confirm opportunities and gives you insight into how to enter the field.

- Be flexible on entry points. Your first role in a new arena might be junior or sideways to your last one—that's okay. If it's a growing field, you can rise quickly. Focus on getting your foot in the door where growth is strongest. Once inside, you can climb.

- Emphasize your unique value. When you go for a new opportunity, highlight how your background adds a unique perspective. Maybe you're not "the typical candidate." But you bring customer knowledge, leadership experience, or creativity from another field. These could be selling points in teams that need diverse thinking to innovate.

The AI era is still young. By positioning yourself at the frontier, you're effectively surfing a wave that's gaining momentum. There will be competition and a *vast ocean of new problems to solve*. There is enough for everyone who is willing to learn and adapt. Be encouraged by the fact that with every new technology cycle, fresh experts emerge. They often started just by being curious and proactive. You can follow their lead.

Long-Term Positioning

The only certainty in the future of work is change. In earlier industrial revolutions, disruption eventually stabilized into new norms. Today's transformation is different. AI, biotechnology, robotics, and digital platforms are advancing simultaneously—and each advancement accelerates the others. The result is a pace of change with no obvious plateau. What was once measured in decades is now unfolding in years, even months.

For your career, this means that long-term positioning isn't about waiting for stability—it's about learning to thrive in motion. Resilience and adaptability become permanent skills, not temporary strategies. The habits you've practiced in this book—fast learning, smart networking, and applying AI to your workflow—are not just tools for the present, but a way of working that keeps you relevant no matter how quickly the ground shifts.

Build a Career Portfolio

Think of your career as a portfolio. A diverse portfolio weathers storms effectively. Cultivate a broad *portfolio of skills and experiences*. Don't overspecialize to the point that one technological change could make you obsolete. Instead, anchor yourself in evergreen skills and add new ones regularly.

The "blue-chip stocks" of your portfolio. Strong communication, problem-solving, and leadership abilities are valuable in almost any role. Technical skills can change. But your ability to learn technical skills quickly is a lasting asset. Emphasize learning *how to learn*.

Adapt at Speed

Those who can quickly adopt new tools or concepts will stay in demand. Employers increasingly value adaptability and self-management—resilience, curiosity, active learning—just as much as technical know-how (Zahidi, 2020). The half-life of knowledge is shortening; what you learned five years ago may carry less weight today. Continuous improvement is no longer optional—it's the baseline.

Leverage AI and digital platforms to accelerate your learning. Personalized upskilling, micro-certifications, and real-time practice projects are easier than ever to access. Use them to stay ahead.

Future-Proof Your Skills

No skill is truly future-proof, but some have greater staying power. Focus on what makes us distinctly human: creativity, strategic thinking, empathy, and leadership. AI can analyze data, but humans bring judgment, cultural nuance, and original vision. Develop complementary skills—communication, storytelling, innovation, and team-building—so you thrive alongside technology.

Roles like facilitators, strategists, and innovators can't be filled by machines. Employers repeatedly cite these "power skills" as critical for the future of work (WEF, 2025). Pair them with digital literacy, so you can adopt new tools quickly and effectively.

Plan for Multiple Career Stages

Long-term positioning means recognizing that your career may unfold in distinct chapters. Gone are the days of one-track careers. People today average a dozen jobs over a lifetime (USBLS, 2024), and that number could rise in a fast-changing economy. You might have a corporate chapter, an entrepreneurial chapter, a public service chapter, or even a teaching chapter later on.

Don't resist these shifts—plan for them. Envision your career less as a ladder and more as a jungle gym with multiple paths upward. For example, you might use your 30s to gain depth in two industries, your 40s to launch a venture or consult, and your 50s to teach or mentor. There's no single formula but thinking ahead gives you options. Build flexibility—financially, emotionally, professionally—so you can pivot when needed.

Networks That Compound

Networking is not just for job hunting—it's your long-term safety net, brain trust, and community of practice. Keep nurturing your connections through every career stage. As you rise, support others. Goodwill compounds, and many of the best opportunities (especially senior roles or collaborations) flow through people who have known you for years and can vouch for your reputation.

Stay connected. Update others on your journey and take interest in theirs. Relationships compound like interest, creating rich webs of allies and advisors over time.

Resilience for the Long Haul

Long-term success in a fast-changing world requires emotional resilience. Every year won't be a boom year. Industries will face downturns and projects may fail. Those who thrive treat setbacks as learning experiences, not endpoints.

If AI eliminates part of your job, see it as an invitation to carve out a new role that leverages AI. If one company or career path no longer fits, remember you can reinvent yourself—you've done it before in smaller ways, and you can do it again on a larger scale.

Stay alert to macro trends. Regularly check future-of-work reports and trusted sources to keep your perspective current. But above all, trust your ability to adapt. Balanced, proactive mindsets keep you from fear or complacency.

Long-term positioning is no longer about waiting for stability. It's about thriving in motion. Cultivate durable human skills, stay networked, and embrace lifelong learning. In a world where the only certainty is change, adaptability is your edge.

Do This Now: The Opportunity Window

Scan the Horizon

This week, identify one emerging trend (AI-related or otherwise) that could impact your industry. Read at least one report or article on it. Understanding the change is the first step to leveraging it.

Map Your Gaps

Write down three skills or experiences you don't have but that would make you more marketable. These could be technical (data analysis, coding in Python) or soft skills (public speaking, strategic planning). Commit to starting to develop at least one of them in the next month. Sign up for a course, volunteer for a task, etc.

Refresh Your Network

Reach out to a mentor or colleague who seems to be ahead of the curve (someone who's embraced new trends). Ask for a casual chat to pick their brain on how they see the industry evolving. Their insight might reveal opportunities you haven't considered.

Create a "Future Portfolio" Project

Start a small personal project that aligns with where you think opportunities will be. For example, if you're in finance, experiment with a simple machine learning model on stock data. If you're in retail, launch a tiny online shop to learn e-commerce. It doesn't have to succeed commercially. The goal is to learn and demonstrate initiative in a forward-looking area.

Set a Long-Term Vision (with Flexibility)

Take 30 minutes to envision your career 5-10 years from now. Write a short "vision statement" for yourself: for example, "In five years, I see myself as a leader in implementing AI solutions in the supply chain field, known for my team leadership and technical expertise." Don't worry if the target changes. Having a vision will motivate you. Revisit and update it periodically.

Pick Up a New Habit

Choose one habit to keep you future-focused and start it now. It could be as simple as "read one article about future tech every morning" or "each month, attend one webinar outside my direct expertise." Consistent habits ensure continued progress without big pushes.

These immediate actions will help you seize the present and future, bridging your current self with the evolving professional you aim to become.

Make Your Move

Every great career story has a defining moment. Someone decides to leap, to strive, to become more. This is your defining moment. The disruption we're living in, powered by AI and rapid innovation, isn't a threat to your career. It's a launchpad for your career.

The landscape is shifting. As we've seen, those shifts are creating new landscapes rich with possibility. By taking the steps outlined—accelerating your progress in 90-day bursts, embracing lifelong learning, nurturing your network, and staying adaptable—you are turning a potential career quake into the adventure of a lifetime.

The future of work belongs to the curious and the resilient (WEF, 2025). Whenever you feel uncertainty, remember you've equipped yourself with a mindset and tools to navigate change. You won't be caught off guard. You'll be out front, scouting the path and lighting the way for others. The confidence that preparedness brings is real. And you've earned it through the effort of leveling up.

Historically, every wave of progress had its pioneers, individuals who stepped forward when others stood still. They started new businesses, learned new skills, moved to growing cities, or said "I'll give it a try."

They transformed their lives and the lives of many around them. At this juncture, you can be that person. By acting with intention and courage, you position yourself to reap the rewards of this era's opportunities. It could be a dream job, a new venture, or a chance to solve meaningful problems on a global scale.

Your next level career isn't some far-off promise. It's taking shape right now in the actions you take and the choices you make. The window of opportunity is wide open. Step through it with confidence, knowing that you have the roadmap and the resolve to succeed.

You've done the preparation. Now it's time to execute, to trust yourself, to embrace the exciting journey ahead. The world needs people like you: adaptable, skilled, and motivated to make an impact. Go forth and claim your next level career. The future is yours to shape.

You've got this.

References

Autor, D. H., Chin, C., Salomons, A., & Seegmiller, B. (2024). New frontiers: The origins and content of new work, 1940-2018. Quarterly Journal of Economics, 139(3), 1399-1465. https://news.mit.edu

Autor, D. H., Mindell, D. A., & Reynolds, E. B. (2022). The work of the future: Building better jobs in an age of intelligent machines. MIT Press.

Blease, C., Kharko, A., Bernstein, M. H., Gaab, J., Kaptchuk, T. J., Mandl, K. D., & DesRoches, C. M. (2019). Artificial intelligence and the future of primary care: Exploratory qualitative study of UK general practitioners' views. Journal of Medical Internet Research, 21(3), e12802. https://doi.org/10.2196/12802

Brynjolfsson, E., & McAfee, A. (2017). Machine, platform, crowd: Harnessing our digital future. W. W. Norton & Company.

Bureau of Labor Statistics. (2024, January 3). Baby boomers born from 1957 to 1964 held an average of 12.7 jobs from ages 18 to 56. The Economics Daily. https://www.bls.gov/opub/ted/2024/baby-boomers-born-from-1957-to-1964-held-an-average-of-12-7-jobs-from-ages-18-to-56.htm

Bureau of Labor Statistics. (2025, April 18). Fastest growing occupations. Occupational Outlook Handbook. https://www.bls.gov/ooh/fastest-growing.htm

Carolan, S., Wu Martin, A., Gong, C. C., & Borja, S. (2025, June 26). 2025: The state of consumer AI. Menlo Ventures. https://menlovc.com/perspective/2025-the-state-of-consumer-ai/

Davenport, T. H., & Bean, R. (2023). How to build a future-ready workforce. MIT Sloan Management Review, 64(4), 34-41.

Deloitte. (2023). 2023 global human capital trends: Navigating disruption. Deloitte Insights. https://www2.deloitte.com

Deming, D. J. (2017). The growing importance of social skills in the labor market. The Quarterly Journal of Economics, 132(4), 1593-1640. https://doi.org/10.1093/qje/qjx022

Goldman Sachs. (2023, April 5). Generative AI could raise global GDP by 7%. Goldman Sachs Research. https://www.goldmansachs.com

Hu, K. (2023, February 2). ChatGPT sets record for fastest-growing user base. Reuters. https://www.reuters.com/...

IBM Institute for Business Value. (2022). The enterprise guide to closing the skills gap. IBM Research. https://www.ibm.com/thought-leadership/institute-business-value

IBM Institute for Business Value. (2023). AI upskilling strategy. IBM Think Insights. https://www.ibm.com

International Federation of Robotics. (2024, November 20). Global robot density in factories doubled in seven years. IFR Press Release. https://ifr.org

Lauder, E. (2017, March 10). AI will power 95% of customer interactions by 2025. AI Business. https://aibusiness.com

LinkedIn. (2023). 2023 workplace learning report. LinkedIn Learning. https://learning.linkedin.com/resources/workplace-learning-report

McKinsey & Company. (2017). A future that works: Automation, employment, and productivity. McKinsey Global Institute. https://www.mckinsey.com

McKinsey & Company. (2021). The future of work after COVID-19. McKinsey Global Institute. https://www.mckinsey.com

McKinsey & Company. (2023). The state of AI in 2023: Generative AI's breakout year. McKinsey Global Institute. https://www.mckinsey.com

McKinsey & Company. (2024). The state of AI in 2024: Generative AI's breakout year. McKinsey Global Institute. https://www.mckinsey.com

McKinsey Global Institute. (2023, July 26). Generative AI and the future of work in America (Ellingrud, K., Sanghvi, S., Dandona, G. S., Madgavkar, A., Chui, M., & White, O.). https://www.mckinsey.com/mgi/our-research/generative-ai-and-the-future-of-work-in-america

McKinney, S. M., Sieniek, M., Godbole, V., Godwin, J., Antropova, N., Ashrafian, H., ... Suleyman, M. (2020). International evaluation of an AI system for breast cancer screening. Nature, 577(7788), 89–94. https://doi.org/10.1038/s41586-019-1799-6

Microsoft (Tomlinson, K., et al.). (2025). Working with AI: Measuring the occupational implications of generative AI. Microsoft Research. https://www.geekwire.com

Mutikani, L. (2025, September 3). U.S. job openings drop to 10-month low, hiring remains tepid. Reuters. https://www.reuters.com/business/us-labor-market-softening-job-openings-hit-10-month-low-hiring-remains-tepid-2025-09-03/

New York State Department of Labor. (2024). Job Search and Networking: Finding the Career You Love. Retrieved from https://dol.ny.gov/job-search-and-networking

Next Gen Personal Finance. (n.d.). Job search and networking resources. Retrieved Sept 23 2025, from https://www.ngpf.org/

OECD. (2021). Skills outlook 2021: Learning for life. OECD Publishing. https://doi.org/10.1787/0ae365b4-en

PwC. (2022). 24th annual global CEO survey. PwC Research. https://www.pwc.com

Reuters. (2023a, May 1). IBM to pause hiring in plan to replace 7,800 jobs with AI. Reuters Tech News. https://www.reuters.com

Reuters. (2023b, February 2). ChatGPT sets record for fastest-growing user base – analyst note. Reuters Technology News. https://www.reuters.com

Schwab, K., & Zahidi, S. (2020). The future of jobs report 2020. World Economic Forum. https://www.weforum.org

The Future of Commerce. (2024, December 9). Customer service trends 2025. https://www.the-future-of-commerce.com/2024/12/09/customer-service-trends-2025/

University of Maryland, Baltimore County. (n.d.). Networking 101. Division of Student Affairs, Career Center. Retrieved Sept 23 2025 https://careers.umbc.edu/students/networking-101

World Economic Forum. (2020). The future of jobs report 2020 (Insight Report). World Economic Forum. https://www.weforum.org

World Economic Forum. (2023, April 30). The future of jobs report 2023 (Insight Report). World Economic Forum. https://www.weforum.org

World Economic Forum. (2023, May 1). A quarter of today's jobs will be disrupted in the next 5 years [Video summary]. Future of Jobs Report 2023 Key Findings. https://www.weforum.org/videos/foj-job-market/

World Economic Forum. (2025, January 8). Future of jobs report 2025: 78 million new job opportunities by 2030. World Economic Forum. https://www.weforum.org

World Economic Forum. (2025, January). AI and beyond: How every career can navigate the new tech landscape. World Economic Forum. https://www.weforum.org

World Economic Forum & Access Partnership. (2025). Skills outlook: Power skills. World Economic Forum. https://www.weforum.org

Wynants, L., Van Calster, B., Collins, G. S., Riley, R. D., Heinze, G., Schuit, E., ... Van Smeden, M. (2020). Prediction models for diagnosis and prognosis of COVID-19: Systematic review and critical appraisal. BMJ, 369, m1328. https://doi.org/10.1136/bmj.m1328

Bonus Extras

Thank you for reading The AI Career Book. To support you beyond these pages, I've created a companion resource hub with practical tools, prompts, and planners that expand on the strategies in this book.

Inside you'll find:

- **Worksheets** to guide your self-audit and role stocktake
- **AI prompts** aligned to each chapter
- **Planning tools** for your 90-day roadmap
- **Networking scripts** and visibility nudges
- **Trackers and challenges** to build long-term habits

ACCESS THESE TOOLS AT:

https://go.habitkind.store/careerbook

Think of it as your ongoing accelerator—updated and expanded to help you stay ready for whatever comes next.

www.ingramcontent.com/pod-product-compliance
Lightning Source LLC
Chambersburg PA
CBHW060526090426
42735CB00011B/2389